Fantastic Female
Filmmakers

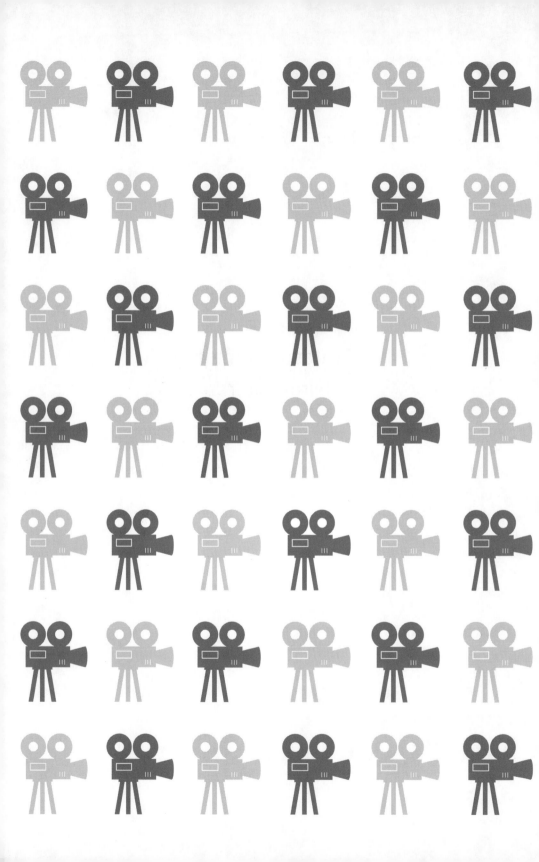

Fantastic Female Filmmakers

Suzanne Simoni

Second Story Press

Library and Archives Canada Cataloguing in Publication

Simoni, Suzanne, 1957-
Fantastic female filmmakers / by Suzanne Simoni.

(Women's hall of fame series)
Includes bibliographical references.
ISBN 978-1-897187-36-4

1. Women motion picture producers and directors—Biography—
Juvenile literature. I. Title. II. Series.

PN1998.2.S45 2008   j791.43023'30922   C2007-906432-9

Edited by Carolyn Jongeward
Designed by Melissa Kaita
Cover photo and icons © istockphoto.com
Printed and bound in Canada

*Second Story Press gratefully acknowledges the support of the Ontario Arts Council
and the Canada Council for the Arts for our publishing program. We acknowledge
the financial support of the Government of Canada through the Book Publishing
Industry Development Program.*

ONTARIO ARTS COUNCIL
CONSEIL DES ARTS DE L'ONTARIO

Canada Council   Conseil des Arts
for the Arts   du Canada

Published by
Second Story Press
20 Maud Street, Suite 401
Toronto, ON
M5V 2M5
www.secondstorypress.ca

CONTENTS

To Rachel and Benjamin – and to my Guy

INTRODUCTION

Filmmaking has been a rocky business for women. It started out well enough. Back in 1896 the movie camera was just being developed, and a few men filmed things such as trains going into tunnels. Meanwhile a woman in France, Alice Guy-Blaché, borrowed a camera from the manufacturer she was working for and made the first movie that told a story. As directors, producers, editors, and writers, women followed her lead and started to make movies. One of them, Nell Shipman, placed a camera in the snow and filmed in the wilds of the Great White North. Right up until the middle of the 1920s, filmmaking was good news for women.

Then in came the "talkies" – movies with sound. Movie studios were born because filmmakers needed sets built away from noise. Not only did studios such as Warner Brothers have film stages, but they also bought distribution companies, and even the theaters that screened the films. Studios didn't have to worry whether theaters would show their movies, because they owned them. Making films became big business. Unions were formed and they were reluctant to admit women. The playful, pioneering spirit of filmmaking disappeared, and women found it difficult to find work behind the camera. Even now, after more than one hundred years of filmmaking, only about twelve percent of Hollywood directors are women, a figure not much different in the rest of the world.

Despite the odds, women have made a huge impact in the world of film. Dorothy Arzner, for example, was the only woman director working in Hollywood when talkies had just started. Sound was captured by microphones placed along the edges of sets. Actors had to lean toward the microphones to say their lines. One day Dorothy had the idea of using a fishing rod to suspend the microphones over the heads of the actors so that they could say their lines anywhere on the set. She had invented the boom mike.

Over the years there have been many more firsts by women – as directors, producers, editors, and writers – all of them impressive. In an effort to narrow down the list to ten filmmakers for this book, we chose women who have had different experiences working as feature film directors. The profiles show the variety of ways that women directors work and cope with the challenge of succeeding in a man's world.

Ida Lupino became a mother figure in order to work with her actors and crew. Deepa Mehta needed bodyguards to keep angry mobs at bay while filming in India. Sally Potter draws on her love of music and dance, Euzhan Palcy uses the setting of her island home of Martinique, Margarethe von Trotta and Deepa Mehta explore the bonds between women and their role in society. Some, such as Martha Coolidge who waited twenty years to direct the feature film she wanted to make in Hollywood, need extraordinary perseverance. Others, such as Mira Nair and Patricia Rozema, make movies on a shoestring and still win awards.

Watch their films (although not all those mentioned in this book will be appropriate for all ages), and as the lights go down, imagine the feeling the director must have. The money has been raised, the script has been written, the sets have been built, the actors have learned their lines. And now it begins: "Action!"

NELL SHIPMAN

1892 - 1970

PIONEERING IN THE WILD

On location in the frozen wilds of Lesser Slave Lake in northern Canada, and just about to begin filming, Nell Shipman crossed the snow toward the snarling dog and shouted, "Keep the cameras going, boys! Do you hear? No matter what happens – don't cut!" Even the animal's trainer was horrified. He was standing by with a gentler dog they had intended to use for these shots. The camera crew kept cranking – which is how cameras were operated in 1919 – as Nell entered the scene and moved her lips close to the dog's snarling face, as if she were whispering comforting words to him.

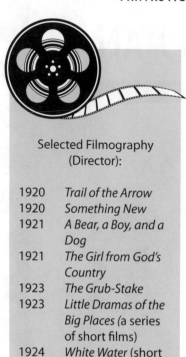

Selected Filmography
(Director):

1920	*Trail of the Arrow*
1920	*Something New*
1921	*A Bear, a Boy, and a Dog*
1921	*The Girl from God's Country*
1923	*The Grub-Stake*
1923	*Little Dramas of the Big Places* (a series of short films)
1924	*White Water* (short film)

The dog looked at her, then lowered his head and allowed her to stroke him. Unknown to everyone else, Nell had been spending time getting to know the "vicious" dog and had become the only one, besides the trainer, to befriend it.

Even as a child, Nell had shown her fearless nature. She was born in 1892 in Victoria, just after British Columbia joined Canada's Confederation. At the age of seven, she visited London, England, with her family. They stayed in the home of her fierce grandfather. Everyone was afraid of him. One day, back at her grandfather's house, after seeing a play, Nell was so excited about what she'd seen at the theater that she broke every rule of those formal times. She approached her gruff grandfather, who was seated at the head of the table, and began speaking to him without permission! Everyone tried to stop her, but she began to act out a part of the play they'd seen. The room fell silent for a moment, but in the end everyone, including her stern grandfather, laughed at her performance. Nell was hooked on acting.

Back in Canada, thirteen-year-old Nell heard that a touring company was auditioning actors at her drama school. She was desperate to act, but her teachers thought she was too young to audition. Nell was tall for her age, though, and she was able to look at a page and remember its contents. The drama school allowed her to audition, and the touring company offered her a part. Reluctantly, her parents agreed to let her go on the road with the touring company.

On the road, Nell experienced both good times and hard times. She learned much about the theater, such as the fact that actors believed if you whistled in the dressing room, or lifted your shoes higher than your head, the performance would be a disaster. More importantly, she learned how to project her voice beyond the third row. However, touring on the road meant virtual starvation – living on coffee and stale donuts. Eventually, her mother joined her on the tour and made sure she was fed properly.

To Nell's delight, being around theaters gave her the chance to see movies that were just beginning to be shown. They consisted of a few minutes of jerky images – called flickers – that were used to make audiences leave at the end of a live performance. Nell thought these shorts, including "tables and chairs walking unaided down streets," were magical. She couldn't understand how people could turn their backs on the flickers. "I could have watched them all day and night," she said.

When she was eighteen, Nell joined a touring company managed by a Canadian promoter named Ernest Shipman. He had been married three times and was thirty-nine years old, but Nell fell in love with him. They married while on tour and moved to California.

At the time, filmmaking was also moving to Hollywood, where land was cheap, sunshine was plentiful, and the terrain was varied. Film scripts of the day were little more than notes on the back of an envelope. Filmmakers would find a place away from power lines, set their cameras up facing north (so the light was behind them), and begin filming, on a modest budget of about $500 (average budgets today are $100 million).

By 1912, movies up to thirty minutes long were being shown on a white screen, which was dropped down on the stage of nickelodeons, where live theater usually was performed. A piano player would accompany the silent film, and the action was explained on written cards that were inserted into the film.

Ernest was busy starting his own film company, but Nell was having trouble finding parts. She gave birth to their son, Barry, and stayed home writing scenarios, or screenplays. In 1913, she entered a contest for film scenarios and won it hands down. "There were no other contestants!" she said. Nell earned $25 for a script that was made into a two-reel film (about thirty minutes long) called *The Wreckers*, but neither Nell nor Ernest was earning enough. They were in financial trouble.

Nell continued to write, and she was offered a job writing scenarios on location in Lake Tahoe for *The Widow's Secret*. It was her chance to earn an income, since she was still out of work as an actress. But before filming started, the leading lady ran away with the director. The leading man told Nell to "take up the megaphone" – the standard piece of equipment for a director. "I was so scared the cast could not hear my directorial cry for 'Action,'" Nell said. As well as directing, Nell filled in for the leading lady. Even two-year-old Barry was in the movie. Although she directed *The Widow's Secret,* Nell was only credited as its writer.

The next year, Nell made a breakthrough. She adapted a short story, *God's Country and the Woman,* into a scenario. It was to be the first feature-length wildlife film in Hollywood. Filmed in 1916, it was about a female heroine who faces adventure in the wilderness. Nell was also hired to play the leading role because she said she could "get around the wilderness without stubbing her toe."

When the film was released, it was so successful that Nell became known as the "girl from god's country." She was offered a seven-year contract by Samuel Goldwyn. It would have brought her fame and fortune, but Nell was an outdoorswoman who preferred mukluks and parkas to the fancy dresses the studios insisted their timid heroines wear. After a lot of soul-searching, she "had the nerve to refuse it." For the rest of her filmmaking career, Nell remained independent – she never lost that courage that she'd discovered as a young woman in love with acting.

Near the end of World War I, Nell fell ill during the world-wide flu epidemic that killed more civilians than four years of war had killed soldiers. She was in a coma and lost most of her hair, but she survived. She had to wear a wig until her hair grew back.

When World War I was over, there was a feeling of optimism in the air and new job opportunities were opening up. Ernest wanted to make a sequel to *God's Country and the Woman,* so Nell adapted a story about a dog that saves the

Nell Shipman was on the cover of *The New York Dramatic Mirror* in 1918.

day. However, in her version, it's a woman who saves the day. The original author was furious. He insisted she change it. Nell agreed, but when the author was gone, she rewrote the story. She wanted to film it her way – the hero who saves the day was to be her character, not the dog.

In 1919, the crew traveled to Great Slave Lake in northern Canada to make *Back to God's Country*. There was no train station at the location where they'd be filming. Nell commented, "We simply tumbled off, cast, crew and the Great Danes, into a snow bank."

It was her opportunity to work with animals – even wild animals – and this was to become a passion of hers. On another

Nell Shipman makes friends with a bear in *Back to God's Country*, 1919.

film set, Nell had once witnessed the crew give an electric shock to a bobcat to make it look angry on camera, and then sedate it with drugs to make it lie still. It died, and Nell cried over the furry body. She made up her mind to do something about the treatment of animals in filmmaking. "I knew it would be a small beginning; but, if I could show these animals on the screen doing their stuff freely, uncaged, unafraid, then a step would be taken, a smidgen of communication established between fellow creatures." During the filming of *Back to God's Country*, Nell used encouragement with her animals, and she succeeded by using techniques such as petting, speaking softly, and the honey stick (a stick dipped into honey to lure the animal to its position for filming).

For two weeks they worked in temperatures that dipped to 50 below, and the cameramen cranked the movie cameras wearing mittens. Ice clung to the men's beards and Nell said the holes in her hut were so wide that "you could chuck a cat through the cracks."

The film featured a whaling ship, frozen in the ice. The second day on location the temperature was 47 below, and the studio carpenters who were building the ship's set gave up and left with their tools. The production manager, Bert Van Tuyle, took over, but suffered severe frostbite. He later had to have three toes amputated. The leading man contracted pneumonia and later died in hospital. The crew worked as quickly as they could, and as soon as they had the footage they needed, they returned to California to complete filming.

One scene required Nell to dive into a pool while being observed by the villain. Although it was a time of modesty, Nell wanted to show her character as being part of nature. She was supposed to wear a pink leotard so she would look as if she wasn't wearing clothes, but it wrinkled when wet. So Nell dove in naked, shielded partly by greenery. Publicity for the movie included the slogan, "Is the Nude Rude?" Brownie, her pet bear, was with her in the scene, and she privately called the scene "In a Dark Pool with a Bear Behind."

Back to God's Country was released in 1920. It was surprisingly modern. At the time, most female film heroines were victims who fainted easily. Nell's women lived in accord with nature and used intelligence to solve their problems, which even included saving men. The film became successful all over North America and made Nell a star. However, her success was too much for Ernest and Nell's marriage, and they divorced.

Never one to give up in hard times, Nell started her own production company with the help of Bert Van Tuyle. She made *Something New*, a film in which she drove a Maxwell car over difficult terrain to escape bad guys. A woman at the wheel of a car was something new – at the time, women had just won the right to vote.

Although Nell was famous, she didn't let it go to her head. One day she entered a country outhouse (or backhouse, as she called it), and saw her picture in the newspaper on the filthy floor. From that moment on, she stopped feeling that having her picture in the paper was anything special. "Publicity was for the bottoms of birdcages and the floors of backhouses," she said. This attitude would serve her well in a life of ups and downs.

In 1920, Nell started work on a new movie, *The Girl from God's Country*. She played twins: one blond and one bru-

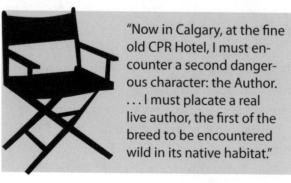

"Now in Calgary, at the fine old CPR Hotel, I must encounter a second dangerous character: the Author. . . . I must placate a real live author, the first of the breed to be encountered wild in its native habitat."

nette. She would do a scene as one twin, then roll back the film stock and reshoot it as the other twin, on the other side of the screen. Most of all, she needed to feel that each twin was different, from the inside out. Every time she switched roles, she would start all over with new makeup.

The Girl from God's Country opened in Los Angeles at a gala premiere in a theater with a large Wurlitzer organ playing the score. Nell described it as a "real sockeroo, twelve reels of whizz and bang." Unfortunately, it was also about three hours long. The studio then cut the film – "entire sequences lopped off the torso and left it bleeding on a sneaky cutting room floor," as Nell said. Furious, she sent ads to the trade papers telling exhibitors not to show the cut version. However, the studios were growing powerful. Many papers were too afraid of studio owners such as Louis B. Mayer to publish the ad. The film was a financial disaster.

Nell introduces a kitten to her bear, Brownie, at her home in California.

This was the time when studios were taking over the film business. Small production companies like Nell's really didn't have a chance. But Nell kept making films.

She wrote *The Grub-Stake*, a love story set in the wilderness. By the time they'd finished filming, Nell owed two weeks' salary to her crew, and she had to edit at night to avoid the sheriff. She did three rough cuts, and then inserted the cards with a line or two explaining the action – the standard way of producing silent films. When the final reels were ready, she packed them in "tins like pie containers" and climbed out the fire escape to avoid her creditors. It was at times like this that her life itself resembled a movie.

Nell poses with her crew on set in "Trail of the North Wind," 1923.

In 1923, she sold her furniture to pay for a trip to sell the movie in New York. This was Nell's first time selling a movie – Ernest had always handled this aspect. At the screening, the film buyers sat slumped in their seats and even talked and made golf dates. Nell thought it was a disaster. Back in her hotel room, everything was quiet. Then the phone started ringing. She told the interested buyers she thought they hadn't liked it. They said, "Don't be silly, Sweetie, we never say anything at a trade showing. You must know that!" Times had changed from the days in 1908, when you could walk along 14th Street in New York City with a film under your arm – and find a film exchange to buy it for ten cents a foot.

Film was Nell's life, but animals had become so important to her that she bought a place at Priest Lake, Idaho – a 21-mile (34-km) snowshoe journey away from civilization, where she could film *and* keep her animals. Her "zoo" was made up of about one hundred animals that she'd collected throughout years of filming. The animals were housed in ten special buildings, not counting the beaver dam.

The Grub-Stake was well-received, but then Nell's distributor went out of business, and *The Grub-Stake* died. Money was tight. In 1924, Nell made the last film her company produced, *White Water*.

Meanwhile, the studios had taken over everything from stages and theaters, to distributors. It meant that they could make a

Nell starred in her film *The Grub-Stake*.

movie and be sure it would be shown in theaters, because they owned them. Small independent film companies had been bought up, or were forced to close. By 1925, Nell's company went bankrupt.

Nell couldn't fight the powerful studios. She preferred the old ways, which included doing a variety of jobs, filming on location, and portraying strong women who were sensitive to nature. The studios now used specialists. They stopped filming on location and controlled costs by using artificial sets and lighting. They didn't even have to worry about weather! Studio heads had become powerful men indeed. And, as for women, a 1920s brochure on careers for women included a full chapter on how to become a film director. But within just a few years, opportunities for women behind the camera had disappeared, and they have never been fully restored.

Nell had no money left. She had written the script for a new motion picture, but couldn't raise the funds to produce it. She couldn't afford to feed her animals and had to sell them to the San Diego Zoo. When it became impossible to make movies, she continued to write scripts. It was much easier to put together words than to put together a movie. Nell took a friend's advice about how to treat the main character in a story: "Get 'em in a tree, throw rocks at 'em, get 'em out of the tree."

Nell went on to marry again and have twins. She continued writing and at age seventy-six completed her autobiography. Although many of her films no longer exist, they remain landmarks of filmmaking. She pioneered animal rights in film and presented women as heroes in a male-dominated society.

Nell said, "Truth is, I was afraid to be scared . . . I am not a brave person. I am a moral coward. I will run madly from angry confrontation with my fellows . . . But from the first scene enacted with the first, free, wild animal, who happened to be a bear, I won out over fear."

IDA LUPINO

1918 – 1995

USING THE MOTHERLY APPROACH

The sign on the back of her director's chair became Ida Lupino's trademark. It read, "Mother of Us All." Ida loved being called mother by her crew, and she used this role as a tool for directing. She said, "You don't tell a man; you suggest to them: 'Let's try something crazy here, that is, if it's comfortable for you, love.'" Or, she would say, "Darlings, Mother has a problem. I'd love to do this. Can you do it?" The special way she talked to her crew may be the reason Ida Lupino was able to direct seven feature films and more than one hundred TV shows, at a time when no other woman in Hollywood was directing.

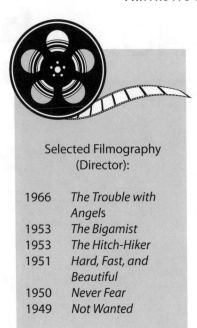

Selected Filmography
(Director):

1966	*The Trouble with Angels*
1953	*The Bigamist*
1953	*The Hitch-Hiker*
1951	*Hard, Fast, and Beautiful*
1950	*Never Fear*
1949	*Not Wanted*

Ida was born toward the end of World War I in London, England, into a family that had long been entertainers – going all the way back to ancestors who were jugglers in Italy in the 17th century. Her father was a famous theater performer, and he eventually added a fifty-seat performance space called the Tom Thumb Theater next door to their home.

At an early age, Ida and her sister learned from their father to sing and to recite Shakespeare, and they were introduced to performing on stage. On the night of their first performance, however, Ida was stricken with stage fright. At the moment when she heard the stagehand call her name and was supposed move into the spotlight, she became so frightened that she ran away and hid. Later, when her father found her, he scolded her, saying "Ida, if you ever let your fellow actors down, dry up in a scene or fail to be a good trouper, deliberately or otherwise, I shall disown you." Fortunately, that never happened. From that time on, Ida emerged on stage and spoke her lines, no matter how much her knees shook.

Ida realized she wanted to become an actress, and so she enrolled at the Royal Academy of Dramatic Arts in London. She would stay up all night memorizing scripts, and in the second term, she gathered her courage to audition for a part in *Heartbreak House* – in front of the renowned author himself, George Bernard Shaw. At the audition, while Ida waited in the heat for her turn, she wiped her damp face. What she didn't know was that the cap to her lipstick had come off and the lipstick had melted onto her handkerchief. So, after using the stained handkerchief, she climbed on stage with lipstick streaked all over her face. All Ida was thinking about was her father's advice to be natural and not to "act." His advice got her through her lines, but later when she looked in the mirror, she realized what she'd done. Shaw, however, called her "the only girl in the world as mad as I am" and gave her the part.

A Hollywood director noticed Ida's performance in *Heartbreak House,* and he asked her to audition for a part in the British film, *I Lived With You.* Ida was cast in the role of a chubby teenage temptress. Luckily, the film was so successful in Britain and the United States that Paramount Studios offered Ida a part in a Hollywood movie.

Ida was only fifteen when she and her mother traveled across the ocean to the United States. But soon after she arrived, she discovered that life was not easy, and her expectations were unfulfilled. When Paramount Studios told Ida that she had to lose weight, she started dieting, and that made her irritable. Nevertheless, filming began.

Then one night a frightening thing happened. Ida woke up in a sweat; she was in pain and had no sensation on her right side from her shoulder to her toes. This was 1934, at a time when more than four hundred people in Los Angeles had polio. There was no cure. The studio had to stop filming, and Ida didn't know if she'd ever walk again. Fortunately, on the sixth day of her illness, while her mother was holding her, Ida began to feel tingling on her right side, and quite soon she was able to move her hand. Slowly, she regained feeling in her whole body, and that night she played the piano again.

Ida's bout with polio had frightened her, and then she heard that her boyfriend in England had died in a highway accident. She fell into a deep depression. She knew her acting career wasn't going well, and she was frustrated because Paramount offered her roles that didn't interest her. She had come to the United States to become a serious actress, but all she had to do in the film *Cleopatra* was to say five lines and wave a palm frond.

Ida made a tough decision – she refused to renew her contract with Paramount, and she gave up her big salary. She planned to look for quality roles at other studios. But this didn't happen, and for a year she was without work in acting. At the same time, she was coping with depression. That year changed Ida; she became tough and more mature. She also fell in love with the actor Louis Hayward, whom she married in 1938.

When she heard that Paramount Studios was going to make a film of the Kipling classic *The Light That Failed,* Ida felt sure there was a perfect role for her. She fought hard to get an audition and succeeded. When the film was released, *The New York Times* raved about Ida's performance: "A little ingenue suddenly bursts forth as a great actress."

Impressed with Ida's performance, Warner Brothers offered her the lead role as a murderess in *They Drive by Night* – and they wanted to lock her into a seven-year contract. However, because Ida didn't want to have the same problem that she had with Paramount Studios, she negotiated and agreed to a one-year contract, from 1940 to 1941.

To prepare for her role, Ida found a method that worked for her. She marked up the script to help her develop her character. But she also discovered that "getting in the mood of the murderer" made it very hard to get out of that mood. She said, "I really think black thoughts, murderous thoughts."

They Drive by Night, her first picture with Warner, was a successful film, and Ida became a star. In public she was mobbed, but fame made her anxious, especially after one of her fans broke into her house. As a result, she became a recluse in her own home. Throughout the rest of her career, she never liked being recognized in public. She said that one of the things she most resented about fame was that you had to "take your own life and give it away to the public, in pieces."

Ida renewed her Warner Brothers' contract with an increase in salary to $3,000 a week. At the time, most working people in America would have been happy to earn this amount in a whole year! However, Warner assigned her a small role that she didn't want to take, and under the terms of her contract, the studio could suspend her for refusing. Ida did refuse, and was suddenly out of work. She turned to radio plays. In the early 1940s television didn't exist, and people would gather around their radios for entertainment.

It wasn't long, however, before Warner Brothers offered her a role in *The Hard Way*. Although the studio anticipated the film would be a flop, to everyone's surprise, Ida won the New York Film Critics Award. This was her first major award, and a big achievement for any actor. Yet Ida had begun to feel bored with acting. She didn't like standing around on set while "someone else seemed to be doing all the interesting work." She decided that she wanted to direct, and she let people know. She put out the word.

In the meantime, "Hollywood's hottest star" lived a private life that was very different from what her public image. One time at a friend's wedding, Ida had an attack of stage fright, like she had had as a child. As matron of honor, Ida was supposed to walk down the aisle alone. But she became frozen with fear while everyone in the church waited, until finally the minister pushed Ida down the aisle. At home Ida planted a vegetable garden and studied medical textbooks late into the night. She joined the Women's Ambulance and Defense Corps.

Then Jack Warner asked her to sign a four-year contract. Ida knew that she would be forced to do all the movies that she was offered, and Warner told her that if she didn't sign, she was finished with his company. But Ida had made up her mind. At age twenty-nine, she refused to sign the contract with Warner Brothers because she needed creative roles, and she

Ida Lupino starred with Humphrey Bogart in *High Sierra* in 1941.

realized that this was worth fighting for. She made a choice for artistic freedom over wealth and security. She cleared out her dressing room. At the same time, she decided to take care of her private life; she had divorced her husband and decided to marry actor Collier Young, or Collie, as she called him.

Although no one would yet hire her as a director, Ida was still in demand as an actor. She accepted a role in the Columbia Pictures movie *Lust for Gold.* But during the filming, she took every opportunity to learn about directing. Often she remained on set after her own part was finished. While many were surprised to see Ida stay in the hot sun, she was watching the director, the cameraman, and crew technicians. This was a time when there was no school for directors, and Ida learned by watching.

As part of her quest to direct, Ida spoke to the famous Italian director, Roberto Rossellini. His view was that Hollywood movies were usually about stars or murders, and he wondered when Hollywood would ever make pictures about ordinary people. This idea struck a chord with Ida, and she decided to do something about it.

In 1949, Ida found a screenplay about an unwed mother. In those days, no one talked about this topic, and Columbia wasn't interested. Ida and Collie, tired of the power of the studios – what they called "front office domination" – decided to join up with a small production company, Emerald Productions, to work on the film *Not Wanted.* To keep costs down, they turned their new home into a film headquarters. There, at Mouse House, as it was called (named after the four-legged occupants that Ida and Collie found when they moved in), they began to have rehearsals and meetings.

Ida set out to find new talent. Among the qualities she searched for, personality was the most important attribute, even more important than looks. She hired a director for *Not Wanted,* but a few days before the cameras were ready to roll, the man had a minor heart attack. When that happened, Ida seized the opportunity and stepped in. During the first week of production, while the director was still weak, but able to watch the action on set, Ida asked his opinion on how to direct the scenes. Then gradually, she became more confident of her own judgment.

Not Wanted cost $153,000 to produce, but it became a popular film that grossed $1 million. Ida did not take credit for directing this movie, but she had other plans for directing. She and Collie fulfilled their dream and formed their own film company, Filmakers.

Ida is credited as the producer on the
poster for *Not Wanted,* although she did direct.

Now that she had opportunities to direct and contribute to the script, Ida found that she could express her need "to make state-

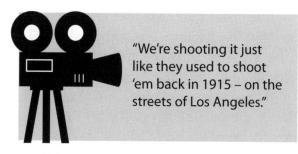

"We're shooting it just like they used to shoot 'em back in 1915 – on the streets of Los Angeles."

ments about herself and the world around her." The women in her movies were as likely to be villains as heroes. Like another pioneering woman director, Lois Weber, who had worked thirty years earlier, Ida addressed topics that others wouldn't touch, such as bigamy, polio, and unwed mothers. Her characters rode buses, and her women dreamed of "Mr. Right," the ideal man – only to discover that he didn't exist. Although her movies didn't have easy solutions, they did entertain.

In 1949, another polio epidemic swept America, and Ida was determined to make a film about it. With Collie, she wrote *Never Fear*, a film about a young dancer who contracts the disease. Collie insisted that Ida direct, and this was just what she wanted. She readily admitted that she never really liked acting. "It's a tortuous profession," she said. "And it plays havoc with your private life. It's about time the screen got rid of the old faces, including mine. I intend to give up acting altogether eventually."

Ida began to develop her own style of directing. "Instead of saying 'Do this,'" she explained, "I tried to make everybody a part of it. Often I pretended to a cameraman to know less than I did. That way I got more cooperation." Also, she didn't show her quick temper on set: "I try never to blow – they're just waiting for you to do it. . ... As long as you keep your temper the crew will go along with you." But above all, her special way of talking to the crew – of being a mother to her crew – was her secret for how a woman could be a director in Hollywood.

Eventually, her manner on set made her so successful that in 1950 Ida became a member of the Director's Guild. At the time, she was only the second woman, after Dorothy Arzner, ever to be admitted.

Movie theater chains didn't believe that anyone would pay to see a movie about polio. So they refused to screen *Never Fear*. Most of Ida and Collie's savings were invested in the film, and even though the reviews were favorable, they lost all their money. Now they were in trouble and in debt, and the turmoil spilled over into their personal relationship; they separated.

Meanwhile, millionaire Howard Hughes had recently bought a film studio, RKO Pictures, and he offered to invest in Filmakers to produce three movies. Ida and Collie, although separated, decided to continue working together on films. But even before they made the first film, they knew they were in trouble. In the contract with Hughes, the fine print stated that Filmakers had to pay for all promotions. As a result, they lost all their profit. Ida had to go back to acting to keep the company afloat.

Ida directed *The Hitch-Hiker*, which was released to great acclaim. But Hughes kept all the profit, and Ida and Collie decided to part company with him. They planned to make and distribute movies themselves.

At that time, Ida's personal life was also changing. She divorced Collie, and soon after married Howard Duff and gave

"Directing is much easier than acting. The actor deals in false emotions, produced on cue. The director has his problems, but they're all normal. He doesn't have to smile into a camera while suffering an early morning grouch."

birth to their daughter, Bridget Duff. But Ida didn't let mother-hood slow her down.

She directed more movies, including directing herself in *The Bigamist*. She was the first woman in Hollywood to attempt self-directing, and it was one of the toughest things she ever did in her career. *The Bigamist* became one of the most acclaimed movies produced by Filmakers, but it earned almost no profit because they tried to distribute the movie themselves. This proved to be a mistake. Filmakers made several more movies, but the company went bankrupt because they couldn't afford the cost of distribution.

When television gained popularity in 1953, Ida changed her opinion that TV was the enemy of movies. By 1955, about 67 percent of American homes had televisions; the cost of a TV had dropped from half the cost of a car to the cost of a set of tires. By 1960, the number of households with TVs increased to 87 percent, and television had taken the place of radio in family entertainment. Ida, along with many others from the movie industry, had become part of a mass exodus into television.

Now that Ida was known in Hollywood as a film director, she was asked to direct television programs. One invitation came from Richard Boone, the star of the popular program *Have Gun, Will Travel*. Ida was terrified, however, when Boone said, "I don't care what you do, just don't ask me to rehearse." This came as a shock to Ida who had been trained – both as an actress and as a director – to rehearse. To begin with, they rehearsed for only one day prior to three days of filming for the weekly show. Then, while filming the second episode, Ida suggested something, and Boone refused. To get over this problem, she told him the camera angle wasn't flattering, say-ing, "Darling, you don't want me to shoot right up your nose do you?" Finally, they were able to get along, because she proved that she had what it took to be a director.

Ida's style of directing became well known. Norman Macdonnel, producer of the television series *Gunsmoke*, said this about her: "You used Ida when you had a story about a woman with some dimension." In the early 1960s, she was also popular as an action director. Some called her the "female Hitchcock," because of her "cool hand with terror." Once, on the set of *The Untouchables*, she directed a performance in a meat cooler: "Peter, darling, hold the knife this way," she said. "And make sure we see the sweet meat hook."

Ida directed her last film, *The Trouble With Angels,* in 1966. Then, by the end of the 1960s, her career as a director was over. Times had changed, and directing had changed. Also, her personal life underwent changes. Her husband left, and her daughter grew up and moved out. This was a hard time for her. "I never expect anything to last," she said. "Neither success nor love." Ida put up a sign outside her house: "Don't Mind the Lion – Beware of Owner."

Ida, seen here in 1979, often wore a scarf
so she didn't have to worry about her hair

Ida continued to act until her last television appearance in the TV series *Charlie's Angels* in 1977. Shortly afterwards her health began to decline and she died in 1995 at the age of seventy-seven.

Ida once said that she was "just a director who tried my best." But when she found her stride as a director, Ida knew there was only one way for her to direct. She said, "I would never think of indulging in what has come to be known as the woman's right to change her mind. As soon as I get a script, I go to work on it. I study and I prepare and when the time comes to shoot, my mind is usually made up and I go ahead, right or wrong." And what she did was no small achievement; Ida succeeded in directing at a time when no other woman in Hollywood could.

MARGARETHE VON TROTTA

1942 -

EXPLORING THE BONDS
BETWEEN WOMEN

Margarethe von Trotta was born in 1942 in Berlin, Germany. Her mother came from a noble Russian family and was determined not to marry, so Margarethe never knew her father, the German painter Alfred Roloff. Her mother later became impoverished, and as a young girl, Margarethe begged on the streets for money to pay for food, while her mother worked as an office clerk. It was a difficult life, but as Margarethe later explained, at least there was no family hierarchy where the father came first. As a result, she and her mother formed a strong bond, and her mother provided

Selected Filmography
(Director):

2006	*I Am the Other Woman*
2003	*Rosenstrasse*
1994	*The Promise*
1993	*The Long Silence*
1988	*Three Sisters*
1986	*Rosa Luxemburg*
1983	*Sheer Madness*
1981	*Marianne and Juliane*
1979	*Sisters, or the Balance of Happiness*
1977	*The Second Awakening of Christa Klages*
1975	*The Lost Honor of Katharina Blum*

an environment that allowed great freedom of ideas. It is no surprise, then, that many of Margarethe's films are about the bonds between women.

As Margarethe grew up, nothing seemed impossible. With this optimistic frame of mind, she went to live in Paris. There, she discovered the films of the famous Swedish director Ingmar Bergman. She spent whole afternoons in movie theaters watching Bergman's films, over and over. She felt connected to them because they portrayed ideas she had been thinking about for a long time. For Margarethe, Bergman wasn't just her idol, he was her soul mate.

In the early 1960s, Margarethe returned to Germany to explore new ideas. She began a degree in fine arts, studied languages, and went to drama school in Munich. And she began performing on stage with much success at the Stuttgart Theatre. During this period she met and married the Italian film producer Felice Laudadio. Eventually, they had a son, Felix. The marriage was short-lived, however, and by 1970 she was divorced.

By this time, Margarethe was not only well-known as a stage actress, she had also become popular as an actress in the New German Cinema. But she couldn't forget the influence of Bergman's films, and she began to think of becoming a filmmaker herself. Her mother had taught her that she was equal to anyone, and that she could become anything she wanted. However, during the 1960s it seemed clear that not everyone agreed with her mother's assessment – female directors in Germany at that time were not making films. When she realized that it would be impossible for her – as a woman – to direct films, she decided to take a detour through acting before trying to direct.

In 1969, Margarethe met director Volker Schlöndorff, a man of great influence in the New German Cinema movement. They were married in 1971 and became a team: she wrote screenplays, he directed them. Her first work with Volker was *The Sudden Wealth of the Poor People of Kombach.*

While it seemed to some that this was the perfect arrangement – with her writing and Volker directing – Margarethe wasn't satisfied. She wanted to direct her own stories, stories about women. Luckily, times were changing. By the early 1970s, the women's liberation movement of the previous decade had begun opening doors for women in Europe. Until then, there hadn't been many female directors in Germany, aside from Leni Riefenstahl, who had worked in the 1930s. Now, other German women began to break into directing.

In 1975 Margarethe took another step toward her dream. First, she wrote the screen adaptation of Heinrich Böll's novel *The Lost Honor of Katharina Blum,* a story about a woman falsely accused of terrorism. Then she co-directed the film with Volker. Although this was an important step, by the time filming wrapped, Margarethe had learned that co-directing was not the same thing as directing. Her role had been to work with the actors, while Volker took charge of the camerawork and the artistic elements of the film. She realized that the only way she could make a film about women who stand for something – who live lives of their own – was to make her own films. Margarethe realized that she wanted to do it all.

She decided to take the initiative. Margarethe approached investors in Germany with a screenplay she had written, based on a true incident. Even though the story was a familiar one, and she had already co-directed a film, she was turned down. She had to face the fact that women still weren't allowed to direct.

Finally, a German television station gave her the go-ahead. If she had known in advance that Volker had spoken to the station and guaranteed the film – even if it failed – Margarethe would have been furious and probably would not have agreed to do it. Luckily for her audience, she didn't know. Volker told her only after the film was finished.

Margarethe's film *The Second Awakening of Christa Klages* was very successful. It tells the story of a woman who resorts to robbery to keep a childcare center open, and it raises questions about the kinds of change that are needed in society. Because of her own experience of being raised by her mother in a one-room apartment, Margarethe understood very well the challenges women face in their lives.

With the success of the film, which she had directed on her own, Margarethe was hailed as a filmmaker to watch. But she didn't let this go to her head. She was already busy thinking about her next project. Her second film, *Sisters, or the Balance of Happiness,* became the first in a trilogy of films about sisters. She had to work hard to raise funds, but the film opened to great reviews.

After the film's release, Margarethe was interviewed on German television, where she spoke about the film, and also about being raised by her single mother. To her surprise, after the program aired Margarethe received a letter about her late mother. It contained details no stranger could have known. "Please," Margarethe wrote back, "if you knew my mother, please tell me everything."

There was a reason the woman knew so much: She was Margarethe's half-sister!

When Margarethe met with Anna Radon, who was fifteen

years older than she was, she felt that Anna was "like my mother's ghost. They looked exactly alike." Anna had been given up for adoption at birth, because their mother was too poor to care for the child. Margarethe had grown up wishing for a sister, but her mother had never told her anything about Anna. This was startling news for Margarethe, who thought that she had known her mother so well. It made her question whether she had known her at all. This, combined with the strange coincidence that her film had been about sisters – one of whom was actually named Anna – was too much for Margarethe. She suffered a breakdown and didn't make another movie for four years.

However, filmmaking was in her blood, and she couldn't stay away from it too long. She began working on a new screenplay. When writing a script, Margarethe's challenge is to develop the characters so well that they become real and take charge of the story. When this happens, the characters begin to live with her night and day. It's a feeling that begins with the screenwriting and continues throughout the time she directs the film. It is as if the characters are "your shadow following you," she says; indeed, it's like "a confrontation with your own shadow."

After so many years of trying to break into the world of directing, it's not surprising that many of Margarethe's films are concerned with the ways that women try to change society. In her next film, *Marianne and Juliane*, the main characters both set out, in different ways, to change society. One sister tries to bring about change peacefully, by working as a reporter; the other sister tries to change society through

"People make me cry and touch me when they tell their stories. There's a jump from being interested to being involved. As a filmmaker you have to be moved."

terrorism. Though the film explored both kinds of change, Margarethe's goal was to promote peaceful change, because in her view terrorists are no different than Nazis.

Marianne and Juliane became known as Margarethe's masterpiece. Through it, she gained international acclaim and, in 1982, she became the first woman director since 1938 to win the Golden Lion prize at the Venice Film Festival.

Within two years, Margarethe had made *Sheer Madness*, the third film in her "sisters" trilogy. Although the film attracted American audiences, the critics – who are a fact of life for a filmmaker – were overly negative, perhaps because they were comparing this film to *Marianne and Juliane.*

Margarethe began work on her next film, the story of a woman who tried to peacefully improve society in the early 20th century. The film is based on the true story of journalist Rosa Luxemburg, who was murdered by German troops in 1919. They shot her twice and then threw her into a canal. Margarethe said that Rosa's murder was like a Grimm's fairy tale where the magic number is three: "They had to kill her three times to make it real, so you can imagine how afraid they were of this small, physically weak person; they were so afraid of her ideas. That's very German behavior." *Rosa Luxemburg* was released to great acclaim, and the film's lead actress shared the Best Actress award at the Cannes International Film Festival in 1986.

"So many women come up to me after seeing my films and say that I changed their lives. It's a fantastic thing if you have a voice and you can speak for others. My films are not only my voice, but the voice of those who don't have the possibility to speak. I take their voice and I make it mine."

During these years of filmmaking, Margarethe and Volker often lived separately while making their own films. Although they continued to respect and support each other, eventually they drifted apart. They divorced in 1991 and Margarethe moved to Italy.

Ready to try something different after making films in Germany, Margarethe made a film based in Italy. *The Long Silence* is about an Italian magistrate who is assassinated while overseeing the trial of members of the Mafia. The magistrate's wife avenges his death by continuing to investigate their sale of weapons; and other widows – silent until then – help with the investigation.

In this controversial film, Margarethe is able to speak out for Italians, who might be frightened to criticize the Mafia. Perhaps because she came from another country she was able to make the film. She had the freedom to film from the unique perspective of a German living in Italy – and not just any German, but the important film director, Margarethe von Trotta.

Margarethe spent six years in Italy then returned to Germany to make a film about the fall of the Berlin Wall. Even though the wall had come down while she was in Italy, she was persuaded to use her special perspective to tell the story.

Her film, *The Promise,* is the story of two young lovers trying to escape from communist East Berlin, just after the wall was built in 1961. As they try to reach West Berlin they are separated and have to continue living on opposite sides of the wall. Over the years they meet briefly, but they can't agree about their life choices or the different politics of East and West Germany. Finally, they meet again on November 9, 1989, the night the wall comes down. By then, they have both been married, and they realize how different they've become. As in many of her films, Margarethe uses history to explain the present, and to try to improve the future. In 1994, *Variety* magazine wrote that *The Promise* was Margarethe's best and most commercial film.

At this point in her career, Margarethe should have been able to raise funds for her films fairly easily. Unfortunately, this was not the case, and like many other women filmmakers at the time, she shifted to television work. It was not until ten years later that she made another film.

During those years she had thought a lot about Steven Spielberg's film *Schindler's List,* which had been released in 1993. Many Germans wondered why a German hadn't made that film – about a good German saving Jews during the Holocaust. But Margarethe felt the film could only have been made outside Germany. She believed that Germans were fearful

Margarethe von Trotta discusses her films in 2007.

of making films about the Holocaust, and were especially afraid to attempt a film like *Schindler's List.* Because Germans were uncomfortable with their Nazi past, Margarethe was reluctant for many years to make the film *Rosenstrasse.* However, she believed that Germans needed to make films about their own history in order to understand their identity as a nation.

Margarethe began working on *Rosenstrasse*, which is based on events that occurred in 1943. At that time the Nazis were in the process of implementing their "Final Solution" – a horrific plan to eliminate all the Jews in Europe. The Nazis were arresting Jews who were married to non-Jewish Germans, and imprisoning them in an office building on Rosenstrasse. But something unexpected happened. The families of the prisoners began gathering outside the building on Rosenstrasse. And even though the Nazis threatened to shoot them, they didn't leave. For nine days the crowd – mostly women – stayed on and even grew larger. This was the first public protest by Germans against the Nazis. At first, the propaganda minister, Josef Goebbels, didn't know what to do. Then, to everyone's surprise, he not only ordered the release of the Jews imprisoned at Rosenstrasse, he even released some of the men who had already been sent to the concentration camp at Auschwitz. *Rosenstrasse* premiered at the Venice Film Festival, where the lead actress won the Best Actress Award.

Today, Margarethe is one of the few women filmmakers of her generation who is still directing. Her most recent film, *I Am the Other Woman*, was released in 2006.

She has become the foremost female director working in Germany. The Italians and French, in admiration, call her "La Trotta." Her films affirm the lives of women, but also raise questions about women's lives, questions that don't have easy answers. Margarethe says that every artist has one theme, and for her, all her screenplays and films are "variations on that one note of internal conflict."

ANNE WHEELER

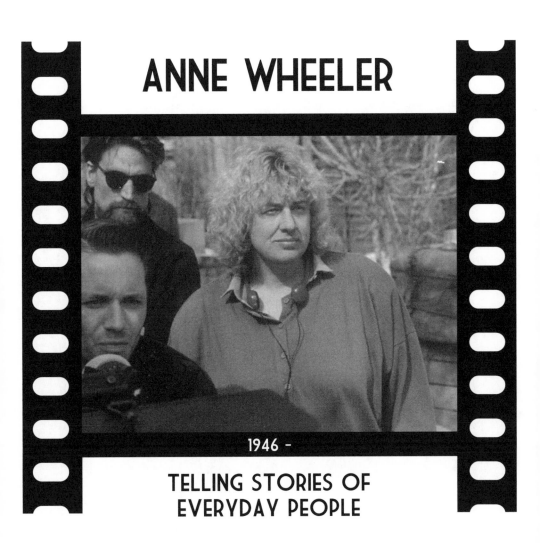

1946 –

TELLING STORIES OF
EVERYDAY PEOPLE

Anne Wheeler was just learning the art of filmmaking when she was asked to shoot a groundbreaking ceremony from the air, for a commercial project. But Anne was afraid of heights. She was using a rented camera and, since she was so nervous, she barely glanced at the camera's user manual before stepping into the plane. Strapped in place with a simple belt used to hold up trousers, she hung out the plane's open doorway and filmed the event.

Back on the ground, Anne thought the worst was over. But she was in for a shock when the rolls of film came back

Selected Filmography:

2002	Edge of Madness
2001	Suddenly Naked
2000	Marine Life
1999	Better than Chocolate
1995	The War Between Us
1993	The Diviners
1990	Angel Square
1989	Bye Bye Blues
1988	Cowboys Don't Cry
1986	Loyalties
1985	"To Set Our House in Order"
1981	A War Story
1975	Great Grand Mother

from processing and she realized that she had filmed everything with the camera held upside down. The only way to watch the film was to stand on your head! While the company's client was on the way to view the footage, Anne got help with bolting the camera upside down on the ceiling of the viewing room. The client never knew the difference.

Anne Wheeler was born in 1946 in Edmonton, Canada. She was the youngest – and the only girl – in the family, and she spent her childhood trying to keep up with her three brothers. After finishing high school, she decided to study mathematics at the University of Alberta, mostly because she didn't want to take labs or write essays, which other courses demanded. During her university years she found time to pursue her interests in theater and music, and to finance her education by singing in nightclubs and performing in children's theater during summer vacations.

Anne worked for six months as a computer programmer after graduating, but she soon realized that she and computers "didn't get along." She packed her bags and set off on a long overland trip through Europe and the Middle East.

When she returned, she still had no clear idea of what she should do. She considered herself a teacher, a photographer, a musician, and an actor. She would have loved to get into drama, but her family didn't consider theater a suitable career. Anne finally decided to become a high school music teacher because that was "acceptable." And, she said, "The idea of being a storyteller had not hit me yet."

Anne obtained a music-teaching certificate in 1969, and then she took off once again to travel for a year through the Middle East and Africa. This time, when she returned to Canada, she enrolled in the masters program in music education at the University of Alberta. And this is when her career in filmmaking really began. She reconnected with nine male friends who wanted to make films about the Canadian West and they decided to form an independent film cooperative. There was no film school in Alberta in the early 1970s, and none of the ten knew the first thing about filmmaking. Anne recalls that this was a time when anything seemed possible. So she threw her lot in with her buddies and they formed the cooperative they called Film West Associates.

Anne and her friends each took turns carrying out the different roles of film production. They learned all the technical aspects, from sound recording, to camera work, to film editing. Sometimes they learned the hard way – someone would mess up by accidentally exposing the film stock, or by filming upside down. But the experience introduced Anne to all aspects of filmmaking, which later proved invaluable in her work as a director. In fact, she later commented that she didn't know how anyone could direct without having had experience in the editing room.

Anne's days were filled with filming, studying music, and earning a living by performing on the children's television program *Wilbur the Worm*. Anne was Wilbur, and as she said, "Wilbur the Worm paid the rent."

Filmmaking soon took over Anne's life. Within a year, Film West Associates was winning awards for documentaries and doing work for the Canadian Broadcasting Corporation (CBC). But after five years and about twenty short films, Film West Associates began to break up.

When everyone went their own way, Anne became a freelance director, working mostly for Canada's National Film Board (NFB). But the travel bug struck again, and Anne took off for India. Traveling always enriched her life and proved to be a source of inspiration. On this particular trip she made discoveries that changed her life and gave her ideas about the kind of filmmaking she wanted to do.

At one point, while suffering India's extreme heat and humidity, Anne began telling someone she met there about her parents, and how they had been born in huts in a country where temperatures in the winter could dip to 40 degrees below zero. From her perspective in India, Western Canada suddenly seemed exotic. Later, this realization had an impact on her filmmaking; and her movies often featured the Canadian West as if it were one of the characters.

On another occasion, while dressed in army fatigues, Anne sat on a curb next to an Indian woman wearing a sari. After

Anne Wheeler on set in *Augusta*, 1976

asking Anne why she dressed like a man, the woman helped Anne put on a sari for the first time. Later, women invited Anne into their homes where she talked and cooked with them. This was another turning point for her. Anne realized she wanted to tell women's stories. She wanted to speak about the important things women have done, and not only the women who have succeeded in a man's world.

Anne knew that "you can't be a storyteller unless you have stories to tell." Traveling provided Anne with stories and made her realize that, for her, filmmaking didn't necessarily have to be about big issues like politics, but could tell the stories of everyday people.

When she returned to Canada, Anne was ready to focus on becoming a director. She continued to work for the NFB, making short films and documentaries, and she helped establish the NFB North West Centre in Edmonton. In 1975 she wrote and directed her first full-length documentary, *Great Grand Mother*, a pioneer woman's story inspired by her own grandmother's journey to Western Canada. It was a docu-drama with scenes that dramatized how tough it was to live in the wilderness.

Anne at thirty

During her years at the NFB Anne got married and, in 1979, gave birth to twin boys. Three years later she filmed *A War Story*, based on the diary of her deceased father. The film, which was narrated by Donald Sutherland, chronicled her father's experiences during World War II. He had been a medical officer associated with the British garrison in Singapore, and had ended up spending several years in a Japanese prisoner-of-war camp. Before making the film, Anne interviewed men who had lived for four to six years in the brutal conditions of a prisoner-of-war camp. Telling her what they had been through, the men had to relive their experiences, which brought up emotions they hadn't felt for more than four decades. Even though it was difficult for them, they talked to Anne because her father had saved their lives. But Anne felt she was exploiting the emotions of these men, and she began to have doubts about continuing to make documentaries.

Despite her doubts, the film won international awards, including the Blue Ribbon at the American Film Festival in 1983. But then the NFB requested that Anne choose either her directing role or her job. It turned out that the timing was right for her, and she decided to move on. She had already filmed extended dramatized scenes in some of her documentaries, and now she was ready to film drama.

She teamed up with a former colleague, Anne Frank, from her CBC days, to develop the script for *A Change of Heart,* a film about a family farm in transition and about a middle-aged woman who must decide between carrying on her traditional life on a farm or begin a new life on her own. *A Change of Heart,* produced in 1983, was Anne's transition to dramatic filmmaking.

"Choose the people you work with very carefully, and try to have them do their job as well as they can, so that their individual styles aren't smothered, and so they don't feel that they're continually doing things that are unnatural to them or against their better judgment."

Anne directed several short dramas, including *To Set Our House in Order,* a half-hour television program based on a short story by Margaret Laurence, one of the icons of Canadian literature. While Anne was writing the adaptation and directing the film, she felt pressure to prove she could do it, especially because she was a woman. "I didn't dare make a mistake," she said.

On the evening that *To Set Our House in Order* was aired, Anne's phone rang at midnight. To her surprise, it was Margaret Laurence herself. They talked for three hours that night. It was a wonderful chance for Anne to speak with the author about the film, the main character, and about what Margaret does with her characters. The production was well received, not only by the critics but also by the author.

While making the transition from documentaries to dramatic works, Anne directed a short drama and an episode of a television show. But she also worked on a feature film. In 1986, she co-wrote and directed her first dramatic feature film, *Loyalties*, about the relationship between a Métis woman and an upper middle-class woman in a small town in northern Alberta. The story Anne wanted to tell was about the power of friendship between women, especially when things get tough. "There are no villains in my movies. There are just people who make mistakes . . . We need to search ourselves and each other for understanding. Humor is good for that."

Loyalties received positive reviews and international awards, and Anne was praised for tackling serious issues. Then she was offered opportunities to direct other films about First Nations people, but she turned them down. She knew that in order to do films with substance and depth, she needed to feel certain that the film would be based on something she understood from the inside out.

That is what she was able to do for her next film adaptation, *Cowboys Don't Cry.* As a Westerner, Anne understood the story of a rodeo star, a man who loses his wife and struggles to build a relationship with his teenage son. For this film, Anne was nominated for a Canadian Genie Award for Best Achievement in Direction.

At this point in her career, Anne began to feel like a real director. She began to find a rhythm in her feature film projects. After six to eight months of writing a screenplay, often in her backyard, she would put on her producer's hat and go out to raise money. Once she had a polished script, she would put on her director's hat, and then look for a producer to take over for the rest of the film. In this way, she could focus on being a director, and also have time to spend with her twin boys.

Anne also spent time scouting film locations. Whenever she knew the location ahead of time, she could work out the camera placement by considering light and composition. She could also plan what was to happen physically and emotionally to the characters in the scene. This is what she called "the dance," and it would define whether she filmed "close together, far apart, sharing a shot, in a wide shot, or in an extreme close up." By planning ahead, she could devote all her time on set to the actors.

Anne knew, however, that no matter how much you planned, there are so many variables during the actual filming that you have to be ready to scrap one plan and go for another. For example, she points out that "maybe your actor is not capable of doing the scene in one shot; maybe the weather changes and you have to move the scene to a different location; maybe you run out of time to do the scene in the way you wanted to do it." It became important for her to have a plan A, plan B, and plan C, and at the same time to keep "the reason for the scene and what it says as the driving force behind decisions."

This kind of flexibility was important during the filming of the feature *Bye Bye Blues*, especially because many scenes were filmed outdoors in the rolling foothills of Alberta. Anne both wrote the screenplay and directed *Bye Bye Blues* – a story

"I can't make films from any other perspective other than a woman's perspective. That's who I am and proud of it."

adapted from the experiences of her parents during World War II. In the film, Daisy needs to support her family while her husband is at war. She becomes a singer in a traveling dance band, but when her husband returns from war, she waves goodbye to the band. It isn't clear whether she gives up her music career or just puts it on hold, but one thing is for sure – Daisy has changed. She knows who she is and what she's capable of doing. As a film director, Anne shows these moments of truth as the everyday moments of ordinary people.

Anne's work as a filmmaker had evolved. Earlier in her career, when she asked a cameraman to film from a certain angle, he would often argue with her. This usually intimidated her. But as she gained confidence, she was able to direct everyone on set, even her camera people, whom she chose carefully. Anne also solidified her approach to directing; rather than being like a general, which most people expected, Anne's approach was motherly and intimate. In her opinion, this method encouraged everyone to do their best and use their talents. On set, she would move quietly from one person to the next, often whispering suggestions or instructions in their ears. Some time later, she learned that the renowned director Ingmar Bergman also worked this way.

Bye Bye Blues was a box office success, received international acclaim, and won three Genie Awards. Even so, Anne faced the problem of finding funding. She knew that if there was too much time between films, her anxiety level would build up, much like stage fright. "Without confidence, an artist of any kind does not soar," she said. "Making one's own film is the best, but it is exhausting, and the time between films can be lengthy."

Television provided a solution to her problem. In 1990, when the film industry in Vancouver was growing, Anne realized that she would have to leave her beloved Alberta. She moved to Saltspring Island in British Columbia and began to direct television series and films for television. At the time her sons were teenagers, and she felt drawn to do a film adaptation of *Angel Square*, the story of a teenager who solves a case that the police wouldn't take seriously.

In 1992, Anne was given the opportunity to direct a two-hour television adaptation of Margaret Laurence's novel *The Diviners*. Laurence had passed away in 1987, but because of Anne's earlier relationship with her, this was a project that Anne couldn't refuse. She had always been able to relate – inside and out – to Morag, the book's protagonist. Anne felt she was the right person to direct this film, not only because as a woman she could bring depth to the film, but also because she could relate to the story's theme of women's struggles for independence and self-expression.

Anne identified very strongly with the film. And, according to producer Kim Todd, she was so focused on the actors during shooting that "a fire could break out next to her and she wouldn't notice." The film won a Canadian Gemini Award for Best Television Movie.

Even though Anne was now considered one of Canada's foremost film directors, she still found it difficult to get funding for new projects. In Canada, she says, there isn't the same tradition of giving filmmakers money as there is in the United States. Despite this difficulty, in 2001 Anne directed *Edge of Madness,* based on "A Wilderness Station," a short story – by another Canadian icon, Alice Munro – about a young woman settler in Canada who marries a man she had never met. Anne's success in television came partly from directing suspenseful films such as *Edge of Madness.*

Anne directs on set in *The Edge of Madness.*

She continued working in this genre, directing episodes of *Da Vinci's Inquest, This is Wonderland,* and *Godiva's.*

Anne believes that each director is different, but that every successful director needs to have compassion and an understanding of human nature. She knows that every life experience can contribute to filmmaking and help make a better movie. She believes that a sense of humor is essential for survival. And she knows that a sense of purpose will see you through difficult times.

For her contribution to Canadian film, Anne has received honorary doctorates from six universities, as well as many filmmaking awards. In 1995, she was made an Officer of the Order of Canada, one of the country's highest honors. Anne appreciates that in Canada women are given a chance to direct. And after more than thirty years as a film director, she mentors young Canadian filmmakers: "I encourage young women to find a story they feel must be told."

MARTHA COOLIDGE

1946 –

PRESENTING THE SURPRISE OF TRUTH

Eighteen years after she had directed her first film, Martha Coolidge still hadn't directed in Hollywood. Then one evening she had dinner with film producer Andy Lane. When he handed her a script – which he said was about girls – Martha didn't think it sounded promising. But he insisted she read it because he wanted her to direct the film. Martha returned home with the script for *Valley Girl* under her arm, hoping she'd like it. To her relief, she did. When *Valley Girl* was released, she said, "I spent twenty years getting to where I am, which is at the beginning of my career."

Selected Filmography:

2008	*Zorro 2110*
2006	*Material Girls*
2004	*The Prince & Me*
2001	*The Ponder Heart*
1997	*Out to Sea*
1994	*Angie*
1993	*Lost in Yonkers*
1992	*Crazy in Love*
1991	*Rambling Rose*
1985	*Real Genius*
1984	*City Girl* (released)
1983	*Valley Girl*
1974	*Old-Fashioned Woman*

Born in 1946 in New Haven, Connecticut, Martha is a descendent of Calvin Coolidge, the thirtieth president of the United States. Both of her parents were architects. Her father owned an 8-mm camera, and he liked filming special effects with it. He would produce a stop-motion racecar sequence, for instance, by stopping the film while he inched a toy racecar a tiny bit forward. Then he'd film again, repeating the process until the car reached its destination. Martha and her siblings loved to dress up in costumes and act in their father's movies. The fun ended, however, when her father died; she was only nine years old.

Martha began performing as a singer when she was thirteen, but she didn't want to get up on stage for high school drama productions. Instead, she wanted to watch from the audience and this is when she began to direct. It felt natural to her to be thinking about the play and how to help the actors make it better. The experience was a revelation for her, and made her feel as if she'd found her home. Yet at the time, it didn't occur to her that directing could be her life's work.

Martha continued acting and singing, and enrolled at the Rhode Island School of Design, where she had the opportunity to make a short film. By the time she had finished it, she realized that "this is what I was meant to be." She continued making movies, and during most of her senior year at college she worked on a 16 mm film. Martha credits her mother with raising her to be an artist; she helped Martha believe she could do whatever she wanted, without worrying whether something was considered a woman's job or not.

During her college years, Martha attended a screening of cutting-edge cinema, put together by Willard Van Dyke, the head of the Museum of Modern Art in New York. While sitting in the audience, Martha began thinking about how she could talk to Van Dyke. Despite her shyness, she forced herself to approach him and tell him she wanted to become a filmmaker. He told her that she should come to New York City and join the independent film community – he even offered to help her. Now, all Martha could think about was graduating so she could move to New York.

After graduation, she did move to New York, and she decided to approach some film producers. One of them gave her some advice: "Whatever you do, don't tell anybody you want to be a director," he said. "They don't want you to be a director." He told her to dress up, get her nails done, and tell everyone she wanted to be an assistant. This kind of thinking was common in the mid-1960s. But Martha was determined. She wanted to make movies. She gathered up her courage to show Van Dyke the movie she had made in college. After all, he had promised to help her. But Martha was in for a big let-down. After screening the movie, Willard Van Dyke told her to give up and do something else.

Nevertheless, Martha decided to apply for graduate school at Columbia University. There, she gave her film to the head of the film division, and he liked it so much that he wanted to show it to his students.

Martha started studying at Columbia in 1968. At the time, students were being drafted on campus for the Vietnam War, the rights of blacks were being ignored, and the movement for women rights was still in its infancy. There were large student protests, and eventually the university was shut down. Since this kind of upheaval was erupting on many other campuses in the United States, Martha decided to go to Montreal. There, she landed a job directing a children's program for a television network. She also made a short documentary film.

Martha returned to the United States in 1970 to attend graduate school at New York University. When she applied, she was again told that women don't direct. She was even asked to name five women directors in the world – and she couldn't. Yet she didn't see why that would be a reason for giving up her dream.

By 1974 things began to change for Martha. She made a documentary, *Old-Fashioned Woman*, about her grandmother, and she began to win awards. Van Dyke helped her get a grant for her next film. And then she received a call from the office of Francis Ford Coppola (director of *The Godfather* and *Apocalypse Now*). He had seen her documentaries, thought she was talented, and offered to help her get started. Martha realized she would need to move to Los Angeles.

In 1976, she became an intern at the American Film Institute. She was paid only a small amount, but she was able to observe Robert Wise (director of *Star Trek: The Motion Picture*) during the making of his feature film *Audrey Rose*. However, when her internship was over, Hollywood still wasn't hiring women directors. In fact, between 1966 and 1977 not one Hollywood film had been directed by a woman.

Martha decided to make a documentary film, and then worked on a rock and roll love story for Francis Ford Coppola's Zoetrope Studio. Unfortunately, the company went bankrupt. The only good news was that Martha finally got an agent. The bad news was that after months of introducing Martha around Hollywood, the agent could not find a movie for her to direct.

It was a frustrating time for Martha, but she made a few short films to keep busy and she worked on a screenplay for Walt Disney Pictures. Then, after three years in Los Angeles,

Martha gave up and left without having made a feature film. She moved to Toronto, bought a house, and began directing epidsodes of *The Winners,* a television series on famous Canadians.

During the same period, Martha wrote, directed, and produced the independent dramatic comedy *The City Girl.* While she was looking for a distributor for it, producer Andy Lane screened the film and was sufficiently impressed that he asked her to direct *Valley Girl.*

Now, at last, Martha had her first opportunity to work in Hollywood. And as it happened, it was also the first major role for her leading man, Nicolas Cage. Because *Valley Girl*, a satirical romantic comedy about teens in Southern California, was a low-budget film, Martha decided to keep costs down by having as many rehearsals as possible before shooting began. She also wanted to make the actors feel comfortable and allow them the chance to improvise. Drawing on their own playful characteristics and ideas, she figured, would improve the film. Martha prefers working with intelligent actors who have ideas to contribute.

After rehearsals for *Valley Girl* were finished, she shot the film quickly, in just twenty days. Mostly the shots were done in one take, never more than three. Released in 1983, *Valley Girl* was a huge hit and a financial success. The film earned $17 million on an investment of $350,000.

By now, Martha knew that box office was what concerned Hollywood most. Studios wanted a big hit, and preferably a movie that appealed to

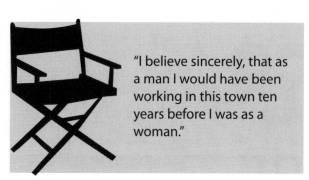

"I believe sincerely, that as a man I would have been working in this town ten years before I was as a woman."

everyone. Of course, "everyone" meant the men in the studios who picked which movies were going to be made, and the men who went out and bought the movie tickets. Martha didn't fit the label "everyone," but she was sure that movies made for women could also be hits.

With the success of *Valley Girl,* doors began opening for Martha and for other women filmmakers. In 1984 *The City Girl* was released, even though it had been two years since she had made it. Around the same time, Martha met Michael Backes. They married in 1984 and had a son, Preston, three years later.

Martha was longing to sink her teeth into something different. One day she received a new script that offered her a challenge. *Real Genius* was to star Val Kilmer as a hero scientist. She liked the idea of directing male roles because she felt she could help men express a more vulnerable perspective through their characters. She also knew that by directing this movie, with its science content and multi-million-dollar special effects, she would be breaking through another Hollywood barrier for women. For her direction of *Real Genius,* Martha won the Grand Prix Award at the Paris Film Festival in 1986.

Martha had enjoyed directing teen comedies, but she didn't want to get stuck making teen genre movies for the rest of her career. At the time, it was assumed that women couldn't make action films, but Martha took on the job of directing episodes of a half-hour cop comedy television series. *Sledge*

"I think there is something uniquely inherent in being a woman in terms of a perspective, but I don't feel that all women are similar in their perspective on the world . . . we will see more interesting female characters."

Hammer! included guns and stunts, and a cop who shoots first and asks questions later. And suddenly, she became known as the woman who could direct action.

By the late 1980s, Martha had gained a reputation and range of experience as a director. However, she was unprepared for the moment when *Valley Girl* was first shown on television. The film had been cut without her knowing. Martha believed that a completed film should not be cut without the director's approval. In France and Italy, she explained, you couldn't buy a painting and then cut it up and sell it. But U.S. law, which is based on English law, is more concerned with property rights than artistic rights. Martha realized then that the director is caught in the middle – what she called the sandwich person. As a director she could help her crew and actors, but she would still have to answer to the company she worked for.

Martha continued to direct for television. And she continued to look for feature film scripts that had strong characters who could face personal challenges and overcome them. Somehow, though, she couldn't seem to find films that she was interested in making.

Then one day, in the early 1990s, she found a coming-of-age story in a pile of rejected screenplays. What she liked was that the story affirmed her belief that "characters are not just good or bad." She directed *Rambling Rose*, a movie for television that was screened five years later to great acclaim. Many consider *Rambling Rose* Martha's masterpiece. The lead actors, Laura Dern and Diane Ladd, both received Oscar nominations.

Even though she is a successful director, Martha finds it difficult to direct for television and still be creative. For example, when Martha directed the television movie *Crazy in Love* (1992), there wasn't enough time to rehearse and prepare shot angles. So for her, directing television is about the subject matter, not the style.

In 1993, Martha began a very productive period of her career, releasing one feature film almost every year. One of these, *Lost in Yonkers*, is based on a Neil Simon play; and it was recognized as a good film adaptation. Another, *Angie*, stars Geena Davis and celebrates the friendship of women through tough times. Martha worked hard to show Angie's good qualities as well as her faults. Knowing that women offer fresh perspectives in filmmaking, Martha felt strongly about including a scene of Angie giving birth, an important event in a woman's life. *Angie* reestablished Martha's reputation as a Hollywood director. Her next film was *Three Wishes.*

In 1997, Martha directed *Out to Sea*, starring Walter Matthau and Jack Lemmon. It is a comedy that goes against the Hollywood norm by showing an older woman as desirable to men, and it entertained audiences around the world. Martha didn't back away from showing characters that "may be misogynistic, immoral or unethical" because, she said, "these are the things in life that we're all dealing with." She wants her characters to be believable. "The core of what's funny is always the surprise of truth," she says. Audiences seem to agree.

Martha was drawing the attention of more than just the filmgoers. For her extraordinary service to the Director's Guild of America, she was honored with the Robert B. Aldrich Award in 1998. The following year, Martha was nominated by the Director's Guild for her direction of *Introducing Dorothy Dandridge*, the HBO TV movie starring Halle Berry. She also received an Emmy nomination for directing this award-winning movie.

In 2001, Martha worked for PBS television on a film adaptation of a novel by the famous Southern writer Eudora Welty. While directing *The Ponder Heart*, Martha wanted to maintain the tone and spirit of the original story. But she also needed to keep in mind the structure of a movie, which has more to do with plot than prose. When it came to the ending of the movie, Martha pushed hard to use the original ending of the book, and she succeeded.

From 1996 to 2001, Martha felt that women directors had had a difficult time. She said, "We do exist, but the hiring of women directors has plummeted like a stone." Then, in 2002 Martha made history: she became the first woman president in the sixty-six-year-old Director's Guild of America. Even so, although more women are becoming directors, not many are making movies. According to Martha, this is because society is stuck in a certain way of thinking about what women do and don't do. She says that, basically, deep changes are needed in our social and personal attitudes, and this is going to take generations to achieve.

After a seven-year absence from directing for the big screen, Martha made *The Prince and Me* in 2004, a popular film shot on location in Toronto and Prague. Then followed *Material Girls*, with Hilary and Haylie Duff, in 2006, and then *Zorro 2110*.

During her career, Martha has worked on a wide variety of films, and she believes there is no one standard way to direct. Talking to young filmmakers, she suggests that they use ideas and subjects they know well. She also tells them that it's important to meet as many people as possible and to study acting.

While her own success has helped open doors for other women filmmakers, Martha warns that being a director has meant giving up a lot, and for her that meant starting a family late in life. Yet she loves the struggle. And even though she has what she calls a "crisis-type" personality, she says, "I really wouldn't do it if I didn't think I was bringing some fun or insight or feeling into people's lives. I think that's what it's all about, our mutual humanity." But she also warns: "The most important thing for a director is to have a good pair of shoes. It's murder on your feet."

SALLY POTTER

1949 –

PUSHING BOUNDARIES
IN THE MAINSTREAM

Sally Potter was dancing "at high speed, often backwards," as she learned the tango in Argentina in preparation for her film *The Tango Lesson*. Since she was going to play the lead herself, she was rehearsing with dancer Pablo Veron. The lessons were frustrating at first. Then she discovered that the only way to follow her partner and move in any direction at a moment's notice was to be completely balanced at all times. Although it wasn't easy, she began to relax and felt as if she were moving "without the need to control" anything. She learned by feel, responding to the pressure of her partner as if the two bodies

Selected Filmography:

2004	*Yes*
2000	*The Man Who Cried*
1997	*The Tango Lesson*
1992	*Orlando*
1986	"The London Story" (short)
1983	*The Gold Diggers*
1979	"Thriller" (short)

were one. And in the process, she gained insight into filmmaking. The "essence of cinema," she says, "is movement."

Sally Potter was born in 1949 in London, England. As a young child, even before she could write, Sally made up stories and told them to her grandmother, who wrote them down. Her grandmother, whom she dearly loved, was someone who said "yes" to life and "yes" to Sally.

When she was fourteen, Sally's parents separated. During this difficult time, her uncle loaned her an 8-mm camera. It opened up a new world for her. For Sally, this was an incredible gift, not just because she could use the movie camera, but because she felt that her uncle (and his partner) had given her – a teenager – the status of a working artist. She used the camera to make "film poems."

Sally Potter loved telling stories, even as a child.

By the time she was sixteen, Sally was making short films. She joined the London Filmmakers Co-op, and studied dance and choreography at the London School of Contemporary Dance. She not only danced in and directed theater productions, she also immersed herself in music, writing lyrics, and singing with bands. For a while, films took a back seat.

It was almost fifteen years before Sally returned to filmmaking. Although she loved music, theater, art, and writing, her first love was still film. Filmmaking offered her a way to combine all of her interests. Sally sees herself as a person who is "one hundred percent filmmaker, who is also from time to time Sally Potter, one hundred percent musician or one hundred percent dancer. It's not about being half one thing and half another."

The fifteen-year detour through music and dance had not been wasted. Sally had developed discipline, the ability to collaborate, an understanding of movement, and a sense of the rhythm of language. She used all of these abilities in filmmaking – in fact, she came to believe that a director needs to perform at least once to know what it feels like.

When Sally finally stepped back into filmmaking in 1979, she made a short film called *Thriller*. It became a hit on the festival circuit and enabled her to raise funds for a feature film about women and gold that she'd been thinking about for some time. She began to write the script for *The Gold Diggers*. She had never relied on a script before, but had always worked things out as she went along, putting it all together in the cutting room. For her short films, this had worked perfectly well. "The idea of drawing up a blueprint in advance and working from that was a complete bafflement to me," she said. But feature films were a different story. Sally began filming *The Gold Diggers*, starring Julie Christie, without a finalized script. The filming was difficult; the editing even more difficult. When *The Gold Diggers* was released in 1983, many critics didn't like it. Sally began to doubt herself. Maybe filmmaking wasn't meant to be her life's work. "The real possibility that I wouldn't be able to proceed took me into a state of almost unbearable frustration and despair," she remembers.

In an effort to figure out where she went wrong, Sally traveled on press tours and attended screenings of the film herself, in order to hear the audience's reaction firsthand. With her background in theater, she loved connecting with the audience. When the lights came on after a screening, Sally engaged the audience in discussion. Such feedback helped, but it would be almost ten years before Sally would make another feature film. In the meantime, she made short films and directed television programs.

During this period, Sally discovered new ways to develop a script and make it come to life. The script became a way to visualize the whole film in detail, as if it already existed before shooting started. Once the script was polished, Sally realized she needed to be ready to throw it away if circumstances, or the actors, or the lighting led her to different ways of making the film better.

In 1986, Sally did something she had never done before – she made a film quickly and paid for it on her credit card. *The London Story* was shot in five days and edited in ten. Sally said, "I remember coming home every night and falling on my bed, and saying to myself, 'I'm happy!'" Although it was a short film, *The London Story* was very important for her at the time. It reminded her just how passionate she was about filmmaking and gave her hope that she had the skills to be a success.

Buoyed by the response to *The London Story*, Sally began a film adaptation of Virginia Woolf's novel *Orlando*. As most screenwriters do, Sally began the process by writing a "treatment" (a short description of the screenplay), and even at this early stage, she felt as if the film already existed: if she looked carefully with her inner eye, she could record what she saw.

In a process that took four years, she transformed the spirit of the novel into a story that could work on screen.

Tilda Swinton (who later played the White Witch in *The Chronicles of Narnia: The Lion, the Witch and the Wardrobe*) agreed to play the lead role of Orlando, and she was a big help. For four years, she came faithfully to Sally's apartment to read each draft of the script out loud. Sally said that it was a four-year period of rehearsing, which they needed.

The story follows Orlando, who, over a period of four hundred years of British history, is first a man and then a woman. At first, Sally wasn't sure how to show this change from man to woman. Then it came to her. She decided that, at the moment of change, she would have Orlando turn to the camera and say, "same person, just a different sex."

This was breaking the unwritten rule of filmmaking that an actor must never look directly into the camera because it breaks the spell of the story. It's only done occasionally, and mostly in comedy. But Sally felt that Orlando's direct gaze into the camera was "the golden thread" of the film, one that connected the audience, through the lens, to Orlando.

During the shooting, Sally became involved with every aspect of filmmaking. She experimented with the view through the camera. She realized that "framing is the magic key, the door through which you're looking." Her quest was not just to frame a scene, or place the camera in a specific spot. She believed that only one perfect shot was possible, and her driving visual obsession was to find that shot. Although she didn't always know what she wanted, Sally

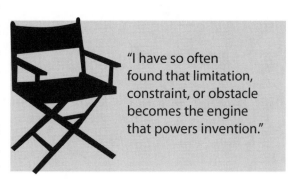

"I have so often found that limitation, constraint, or obstacle becomes the engine that powers invention."

and the cameraman worked with a monitor: "every frame was adjusted – up, down, right, left – until there was a frame which he and I agreed was *the* frame."

Since music is such an important part of her life, Sally also worked with composer David Motion to write the soundtrack.

Once filming was over, Sally spent days in the editing suite. Part of the challenge during filming had been to show that many decades had passed. One way to do this occurred to her in the editing room. At one point, Orlando enters a maze in the 18th century, and when she comes out, she's wearing a different dress, a style from the Victorian Age of the 19th century.

When *Orlando* was complete, Sally dedicated the film to Beatrice Quennell, her supportive grandmother and "great encourager," who had died before the film was finished. But Sally had continually felt her presence during the process of production.

Orlando was released to wide acclaim in 1992. The film received two Academy Award nominations and a standing ovation at the Sundance Film Festival. Most important to Sally, however, is that *Orlando* empowered audiences: it gave them hope that they could bring about positive change.

Sally spent a year traveling with her film on a press tour. After it was over, she returned home with the idea of making

"You can write a scene for 500 people on the ice in brilliant sunshine and on that day it's snowing . . . You have to start incorporating the notion of snow into the scene in a way that wasn't there before. That's the kind of improvisation I'm talking about . . . You use the luck, sometimes, of things as part of your creative muscle."

a film about dance. That's when the idea for *The Tango Lesson* took hold. Sally flew to Argentina.

She took lessons, rehearsed, and then began shooting. In the film, Sally plays a filmmaker who speaks English and is fluent in the language of images; in contrast, Pablo Veron plays an Argentinean dancer who speaks Spanish and is fluent in the language of movement. At first they're unable to communicate, but they find a common language in the tango. An immensely popular film, *The Tango Lesson* premiered at the Venice Film Festival.

For the next three years, Sally worked on *The Man Who Cried*, starring Johnny Depp, Christina Ricci, and Cate Blanchett. It was released in 2000 to mixed reviews.

Like many filmmakers, Sally was deeply affected by the 9/11 attack on New York's World Trade Center. She was left "with a feeling of urgency, impotence, helplessness" and also an urge to do something about it. She wanted to make sense of the destruction and to explore ways to make "the enemy" human. She began to draft a script for *Yes* – a love story between a woman from Ireland and a man from the Middle East – different parts of the world where there had been recent wars over religion.

It wasn't easy to show the enemy as human. Sally felt that the idea of "the enemy" was complicated: often the enemy was just an invention to help justify war and keep people in a state of fear. In the film, she created two characters who learn respect by listening, even though they're different.

Listening became an important part of the film, and maybe that's why Sally decided to write the script for *Yes* entirely in verse. Sally calls it a long song, and she compares it to rap and hip hop. She says there's something "very playful about words arranged not just for their meaning, but also for their sound and rhythm." Like most writers, she struggled with the ending. The story was inspired by a horrific event, but Sally wanted it to end with hope, with something that energized people and made them think creatively, instead of with despair.

Once filming began, Sally worked with her actors so that they wouldn't feel stiff when they said their lines. Instead of focusing on the poetry of the script, she suggested they concentrate on the meaning and emotion.

As with her other films, Sally had definite ideas about the soundtrack. She composed and produced it using the music of Eric Clapton, B.B. King, and Brahms, all in similar keys.

Sally had taken a big chance producing a feature film spoken entirely in verse. And when *Yes* was released, some critics loved it; others did not. But whether they liked the film or not, most agreed that it was a daring work that pushed the boundaries of filmmaking. They recognized her as a filmmaker who is experimental in her vision, even when she is producing mainstream films.

Looking back, Sally feels she has always been a loner, even an outsider. Often the only female, she has never felt part of a community of filmmakers – partly because, as Sally puts it, most male filmmakers "have the buddy thing going."

Whenever she finishes a film, Sally looks forward to writing again – getting back to the simplicity of a blank sheet of paper and sharpened pencil. That, for her, is exciting. And that's when she is likely already thinking of taking her next risk. For Sally, repeating what she's done just isn't fun.

Asked to give advice to young filmmakers, Sally says that it's important to be strong, take risks and not to give up or play safe. "Do what you really believe in," Sally says. "Life is too short to do it for money or for anything else."

DEEPA MEHTA

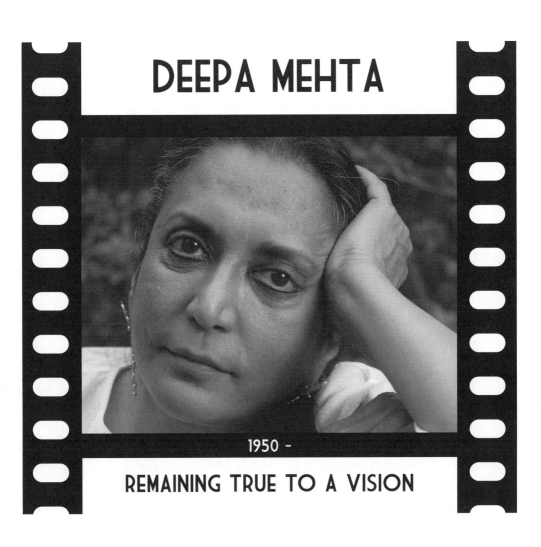

1950 -

REMAINING TRUE TO A VISION

Even as a baby, Deepa Mehta found herself living between two worlds. She was born in 1950 in Amritsar, India – right on the border between Pakistan and India. Her parents had only recently moved there, fleeing the violence that was occurring between these two countries, following the historic partition of India in 1947.

It wasn't until she was six that Deepa saw her first movie. It made her cry because she couldn't understand why she couldn't touch the people, or smell them. Her father, who owned the theater, took her up to the projection room and let

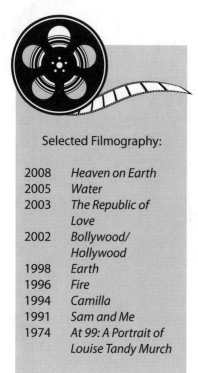

Selected Filmography:

2008	*Heaven on Earth*
2005	*Water*
2003	*The Republic of Love*
2002	*Bollywood/Hollywood*
1998	*Earth*
1996	*Fire*
1994	*Camilla*
1991	*Sam and Me*
1974	*At 99: A Portrait of Louise Tandy Murch*

her touch the strip of film. Then he led her down the aisle to touch the screen. She put her tiny hand on the spot where someone was walking. For Deepa, film was magic.

From then on, Deepa and her friends would run to the theater after school and watch movies for free. Often they caught the end of one movie and the beginning of the next. Still, Deepa wasn't thinking about becoming a filmmaker. If anything, seeing the ailing people on the dusty streets of India made her want to become a doctor.

Years later, she still didn't want to become a filmmaker, but she didn't want to be a doctor either. Like many students, she wasn't sure what to do. In the end, she graduated from the University of Delhi with a degree in philosophy. While she was in what she called this "snob phase," a friend told her that if she didn't put her imagination to work, she was doomed.

One evening at a party, someone told her about a job at a documentary film company. With nothing else to do, Deepa took her first job in film – serving coffee and tea. Eventually she became more involved: she learned how to record sound, edit a movie, and gaze through the eye of a movie camera. Her interest in filmmaking was beginning to take hold.

One day while doing some research at the High Commissioner's house in Delhi, Deepa met Paul Saltzman, a Canadian filmmaker. They found common ground in their passion for film, fell in love, and married.

In 1973, Deepa stepped onto a plane with Paul, destined

for Canada. Together with Deepa's brother, they founded Sunrise Films in Toronto and began making documentary films and television programs. Although her new life in Canada had its challenges, Deepa was doing the work she loved, including scriptwriting, editing, and producing. A year later she made her Canadian directorial debut *At 99: A Portrait of Louise Tandy Murch* was an acclaimed short documentary about a ninety-nine-year-old woman who lifted herself into a headstand three times during filming – just because she could!

Over the next few years, Deepa and Paul produced a documentary film series called *Spread Your Wings*, about children doing crafts. In addition, Deepa directed episodes of the television series *Danger Bay*. As time went on, though, she longed to try something more creative. What she really wanted was to direct a feature film.

Deepa got her first chance in 1987, as the co-director of *Martha, Ruth and Edie.* By invitation, the film was screened at the Cannes International Film Festival, and it won an award at the International Film Festival in Florence the following year.

Ready for more challenges, Deepa read a screenplay called *Sam and Me*. When she finished reading it, she felt that if she didn't make this film she would die. It was about a young man from India who arrives in Canada, and is pressured into taking a job caring for an aging Jewish man. The two form a friendship, but are forced apart by the families.

"I want to be free to explore everything, even something that doesn't make me look too good. If I want to explore it, it has to come from a place of honesty and not what is expected of me because I happen to be non-white or a woman."

Deepa loved the story, but had practically no money to film it. She worked on a small budget and kept the locations to a minimum. Again, she was invited to screen *Sam and Me* at the 1991 Cannes International Film Festival. The judges loved her film so much that Deepa received an honorable mention for the Caméra d'Or Prize.

As so often happens, just when the creative side of her life was successful, the personal side suffered. Deepa and Paul had been living apart for a few months, and in Cannes their marriage ended. They asked their eleven-year-old daughter, Devyani, to choose with whom she would like to live, and she chose her father. This was extremely difficult for all three of them.

Soon after she returned to Toronto from Cannes, Deepa received a phone call from George Lucas, the director of *Star Wars* and the *Indiana Jones* series. Deepa stared into the receiver with disbelief and said "Ha, ha, very funny." She hung up. She was sure someone was playing a joke on her. Luckily Lucas called back. He wanted Deepa to direct an episode of the television series *The Young Indiana Jones Chronicles*. All of a sudden Deepa was no longer a director struggling to work on a tiny budget.

Directing *The Young Indiana Jones Chronicles* opened doors for Deepa. Soon she was asked to direct *Camilla*, a big-budget feature with a big cast and famous actors, including Jessica Tandy and Bridget Fonda. The story appealed to her because of the relationship it depicted between two women of different generations. At $11 million, the budget for this film was the largest ever provided for a woman director in Canada in the early 1990s. Although Deepa had worked with a large cast on *The Young Indiana Jones Chronicles*, she was still a bit anxious. Two things made it easier for her: Deepa read the script more than a hundred times, and she rehearsed with the actors for three weeks. During that time, she discussed with them how their characters changed throughout the story (the arc) and why the characters do what they do (their motivation).

The first day of shooting was overwhelming. She'd never seen so many people on a film set before, but she soon got used to it. Filming went well, and after it was over she worked with the editors in post-production to shape the scenes.

When the final cut was screened for film executives, they were silent. Deepa wasn't sure why, but she found out later, when the film was released in theaters. Apparently the executives didn't like the film. *Camilla* had been re-edited. The final film was not at all like the one Deepa had made. "I learned the hard way, but it was a good lesson," she said. Deepa promised herself that she would never do another film without having full control over the final cut.

Since then she's been true to her word. But in order to have that amount of control over a film, she's had to wear the hats of writer, director, and producer. For Deepa, this meant writing and directing a screenplay, and finding her own funding. It took three years to bring her next film to the screen. *Fire* is the story of two sisters-in-law, in India, who are trapped in arranged marriages and who turn to each other for comfort. It was the first of many films that gave a voice to women in India who had no voice. *Fire* was released in 1996 and won many awards, but it also ignited controversy.

When *Fire* opened in India, theaters were firebombed by extremist groups, and Deepa's life was threatened. She was not prepared for the violence that blazed. She said, "I had never seen so many explosive males and so many jubilant women in one place, all ready to have a fist fight in order to support their particular view of *Fire*. Finally, the police appeared, tempers cooled, and I was escorted to the safety of my hotel." While the film was shown in theaters around the world, Indian authorities ordered that the film no longer be shown in Indian theaters – for public safety reasons. It was withdrawn from Indian theaters.

Despite the violence, something unexpected happened. South Asians began talking about the idea that women have choices. Deepa commented, "You do a film and then you hope people will go and see it. But you don't expect that it might, at least have the potential perhaps, to bring about change, which they feel is needed in this society. And that's what happened in *Fire.*"

Deepa was able to continue filmmaking in safety – from the distant shores and the perspective of Canada. After co-directing another episode of *The Young Indiana Jones Chronicles*, she began writing another screenplay. *Earth* was to be the second, after *Fire*, in a trilogy. "Surely the point about traditional values is that they have to be questioned all the time," Deepa said. "Otherwise, we'll be stuck; there'll never be any change. We would just accept things the way they were."

Earth was based on Bapsi Sidwa's novel *Cracking India*, in which the friendship between Hindu, Muslim, and Parsee students is destroyed by the violence of partition in 1947. This was a theme that Deepa knew about – from the time of her birth. Unlike *Fire*, her film *Earth* was screened throughout India without any violence. It even became India's entry for the 1999 Academy Awards.

Unfortunately, *Water* – Deepa's final film of the trilogy – brought about even more controversy than *Fire*. Deepa wrote the screenplay about an eight-year-old girl who marries an elderly man in an arranged marriage. When her husband dies, according to tradition up to the early 20th century, the girl must go to a home to live the rest of her life with other widows.

Rehearsals began in Varanasi, India, and the sets were built. But before a single scene of *Water* had been filmed, trouble began. Rumors about the film had been circulating in the city and soon an angry crowd gathered outside the studio.

As the crew heard shouting beyond the wall around the set, rioters set fire to an effigy (a model) of Deepa and her actors.

"If people can see minorities as real human beings, complexities, flaws and all, then maybe we'll all be able to talk to each other."

Things got even worse. The next day the crew was told that 10,000 people were protesting the film. Deepa had to have bodyguards to protect her. Investors who had put money into the film wanted filming to stop. But on the bright side, the cast and crew, most of whom had worked with Deepa on films before, offered to work for free. George Lucas published a full-page ad in Hollywood, saying he supported Deepa.

Even with the support of so many people, Deepa faced unrest. The sets were attacked and thrown into the Ganges River, causing half a million dollars in damage. The Indian government didn't want any more violence, and made it impossible for filming to continue. In the end, Deepa had to give up.

Deepa had no film, and had used up all the funds she'd raised. She returned to Toronto. "Suddenly I was no longer just a filmmaker but a controversial filmmaker, which is very scary." Over the next three months, Deepa wondered if she'd ever make a film again. Then she sat down at her kitchen table and began to write a comedy. "They say that comedy is the public face of a private tragedy. And I think that's really true. That which doesn't kill you makes you stronger."

Her comedy, *Bollywood/Hollywood*, is about an Indo-Canadian family that insists their son follow tradition and get married before his sister does. The film follows the style of India's Bollywood films, which are immensely popular. More

Deepa Mehta attends the gala screening of her film *The Republic of Love*.

than five hundred of these films are made in India each year – more than in Hollywood! In this comedy Deepa wanted to ask, "Where does one's own voice stop and the baggage of tradition begin?"

Bollywood/Hollywood was chosen to open the Toronto International Film Festival and it became one of the most successful Canadian films ever made. This achievement helped Deepa feel better about her failure to film *Water*, but she was still looking for ways to make that film. She couldn't obtain a permit to film in India because the government was afraid that more violence would break out. While she tried other ideas, she began working on two other projects, *The Republic of Love*, based on a Carol Shields' novel, and *Let's Talk About It*, a documentary about domestic violence, written from the perspective of children. Meanwhile, Deepa managed to patch together $5 million from investors for *Water*. But even when she added the savings from her own house, she didn't have enough.

Then she found a location outside India. A river on the island of Sri Lanka (off the southeast coast of India) could be made to look like the Ganges, by building steps, or *ghats*, down to the water. Deepa still didn't have enough money, and she wondered how they could avoid the violence. But she wanted to begin.

Other challenges remained. In the four years that had passed, the eight-year-old actor who was to play the lead had grown up so much that she looked too old for the part. Deepa had to find a new child actor, but she was having no luck. Then a Sri Lankan woman brought her daughter in. Deepa felt she was perfect for the part, but the girl didn't speak Hindi, the language *Water* was to be filmed in. As it turned out, the girl had a gift for languages and was able to memorize the lines, even though she didn't know what each word meant. Deepa felt it was time to begin.

To disguise the fact that she was filming the controversial *Water*, Deepa changed the film's name to *Full Moon* during shooting. Her daughter, Devyani, joined her on set as the photographer. They had not spent much time together since Deepa's divorce. Now Devyani was twenty, and they had a chance to get to know each other again.

Filming went well, although there were still challenges. The multinational crew was not prepared for the monitor lizards that lurked in a swamp nearby, or the twenty-foot-long python that enjoyed the warmth of the sun on the newly built ghats.

Then Deepa fell sick with a high fever. The rest of the crew carried on with a scene or two while Devyani cared for her mother. A grateful Deepa was soon back on set, happy to have her daughter close to her again. To cement their relationship even more, they went on a holiday together when filming was complete.

The 2005 Toronto International Film Festival Gala – a special screening for films – opened with *Water*. And in 2007, the film Deepa had worked so long and hard to make was nominated for an Academy Award.

Because her life has been lived between two countries, Deepa has made films that show many points of view. For a long time she felt like an outsider in both India and Canada. Now she feels it's not about the labels that are put on you, it's about being yourself. "I don't consider myself Canadian or Indian; I consider myself Deepa." Her next film, *Heaven on Earth*, is being shot in Canada and India, but promises to be a "Deepa" film.

Deepa's advice to anyone who wants to become a film-maker is to write what you want and to write because you want to. "I've been in that space where I've said, 'I'll make a compromise,' and, luckily, I didn't. I don't regret it. It makes it tougher, but don't make that compromise . . . that's saying goodbye [to your vision]."

EUZHAN PALCY

1958 –

CHALLENGING ASSUMPTIONS AND STEREOTYPES

Growing up on the Caribbean island of Martinique, Euzhan Palcy went with her family to the cinema every Sunday after church. By the time she was ten years old she had decided she wanted to become a filmmaker: "I made a kind of wish. I said I have to be a filmmaker. I have to talk about my people. I have to show what black actors can play, and to show the real image of us." More than anything, she wanted to break down stereotypes.

Euzhan was born in French-speaking Martinique, in 1958. Her father, who worked in a pineapple factory, had been forced

Selected Filmography:

2008	*Midnight's Last Ride*
2001	*The Killing Yard*
1997	*Ruby Bridges*
1993	*Siméon*
1989	*A Dry White Season*
1983	*Sugar Cane Alley*
1982	*The Devil Workshop*
1975	*The Messenger*

to quit school when he was young in order to support his family. He used to say that he wasn't rich, but that he wanted to give his six children the best gift he could, which was to let them study. In a large family, Euzhan didn't have much privacy or time to herself, but whenever she had time after finishing her chores, she would write stories and plays to entertain her family.

When she was fourteen years old, she made her first "movie." She took a paper roll from a calculator and drew the characters – the actors – which she cut out and attached to a stick. She shone a light through the cutouts, creating a shadow play that told a story. Then she acted all the parts.

At seventeen, she began working for the French National Radio and Television station in Fort-de-France, the capital of Martinique. Even though she had never been trained in filmmaking, and no film had ever been made about Martinique, she wanted to make a movie. When she asked the head of the television station for a chance to do this, her idea was turned down. However, Euzhan said, "I won't stop. I won't give up. I don't know what that means. I fight and I move forward." She explained that when you are relentless, you achieve something in the end. And because she persisted, Euzhan directed *The Messenger,* a story she had written for the Martinique television station. Many people were excited about the movie. Some contributed funds and others worked for free. This was first time that the people of Martinique saw themselves on film, speaking in Creole.

After her experience making *The Messenger*, Euzhan

decided to write a screenplay. She had the idea to base her screenplay on the book *Sugar Cane Alley*, written by the Martinique author Joseph Zobel. In Martinique, a French-speaking country, most of the available books were about France. *Sugar Cane Alley* is the story of a black family living on a Martinique sugar cane plantation. It was the first book that Euzhan had ever read about her country as seen through the eyes of a black child.

Euzhan ordered books on screenwriting from Paris and set out to write the screen adaptation of Zobel's book. But the writing process was difficult, and she realized that she could not learn everything she needed to know from books. She thought about going to Paris to study, but Paris was 3,000 miles (5,000 km) away. Her father, who had always supported the idea of education for his children, encouraged her to go. Even though he worried about her as a young woman on her own and far away, the only thing he recommended was that she study French literature, in case she needed something to fall back on if filmmaking didn't work out for her.

In 1975, Euzhan left Martinique to study at the Sorbonne in Paris. She took classes in art, French literature, theater, and archeology. At the same time, she continued to work on her screenplay based on *Sugar Cane Alley* – and she wrote to Joseph Zobel. He was surprised to learn that a young woman was interested in adapting his book into a film. But he offered to help her: he gave her the screenplay rights for free, and later he played the part of a Catholic priest in the film.

Euzhan started to gain experience in the film industry by working as an assistant editor for African filmmakers. When she realized she needed to learn more about the technical aspects of filmmaking, she applied to the Louis Lumière School of Cinema, and she passed the difficult entrance exam. There, she mastered camera techniques and earned a degree in film, as director of photography.

As luck would have it, Euzhan happened to meet Laura Truffaut, the daughter of French film director François Truffaut. Euzhan told Laura about her script, and Laura was so interested that she offered to read it and – if she liked it – pass it along to her father. A few weeks later, Euzhan received a phone call from the famous film director. "He called me! I couldn't believe it. *Truffaut* called *me*," she recalled. "They loved my script. He showed me how to rework it."

Truffaut gave Euzhan the courage to continue. But it took her three more years to raise the money needed to make the film. During those years Euzhan directed and produced a comedy short called *The Devil's Workshop*. And she tried to find a French producer for her film.

Although Euzhan met with one producer after another, it was very hard to grab their interest. First of all, Euzhan was young, a woman, and black. Secondly, there were no stars associated with her film. Euzhan explained to each producer that even though *Sugar Cane Alley* had black people in it, the film wasn't about color. It was a universal story, concerned with passion, struggle, love, and dreams. In many ways, it reflected Euzhan's struggle to bring her story to the screen. Finally, she found a producer who believed in the film and wanted to help her make it.

When filming began in Martinique, many people gathered to watch. It was exceptional for them to see a black filmmaker – and a woman, no less – in charge of a crew of many races, and to watch her make the first feature film about their tiny island of Martinique.

The islanders also came to see the screening of the film. After he saw the film, one old man said, "Now I can die happy." Some years later, Euzhan said that the best compliment she ever received was from "one of my own, who simply said, 'I saw your work and it changed me.'"

Sugar Cane Alley was not only popular in Martinique,

it was successful at the Venice Film Festival in 1983. The film won the Silver Lion Award for Best First Feature Film, the Best Lead Actress Award, and three

"I didn't want to be type-cast, nor did I want to be used – putting my name on everything to advance someone else's agenda. That's why I don't have a lot of films."

other awards. And in France, Euzhan's film captured the Cesar Award (equivalent to an Academy Award) for Best First Feature Film. In the United States, Robert Redford admired *Sugar Cane Alley* so much that he asked Euzhan to attend the 1984 Sundance Director's Lab. Redford, who became her "American godfather," helped Euzhan bring her next movie to the screen.

At the time, black women directors were not invited to Hollywood. Even now, few are offered the chance to work there. But when Euzhan received calls from Hollywood studios offering her films to direct, she declined because the film stories were about white characters. She would reply by saying, "I appreciate your interest . . . but you do not need me to do what your white filmmakers are already doing."

On one occasion, when she was talking to a producer at MGM, she mentioned a project that she was working on. She had written a script for *A Dry White Season,* based on a novel by André Brink. Set in the time of apartheid in South Africa, the story is about the bloody student riots that took place in Soweto in 1976. MGM was interested in her project and agreed to produce the film.

A Dry White Season was a big-budget movie that took Euzhan more than three years to make. And during that time she had offers for other film projects that she had to turn down.

When Euzhan needed to do research, before filming could begin, she encountered the realities of apartheid. She wanted to find out what it was like to live in Soweto – the area of Johannesburg where blacks were denied the same rights that white people in the rest of the city had. So she went to South Africa disguised as a recording artist. But the government found out about her project, and when she tried to return to South Africa to audition actors, she was refused entry. Euzhan had to stay in neighboring Zimbabwe, where they planned to shoot the movie. Her co-producer had to photograph the actors in South Africa and then bring them to Zimbabwe for filming. However, the only way the actors could get visas to leave South Africa was to say they'd been invited to act in a play in England. They flew to England and then doubled back to Zimbabwe.

At the same time, Euzhan was busy hiring the crew. Because she knew how hard it was for a woman filmmaker to bring her screenplay to the screen, she decided she wanted to give women a chance on her set, so she tried to hire women for lighting and camera work. As she told some of her male acquaintances: "Every movie made by a woman is different, of course because women are different from men . . . Brothers, no offense, it's simply the truth!"

Then she chose the cast. Donald Sutherland agreed to play the part of the white South African schoolteacher, a character who doesn't believe that South African authorities are

"Whenever I have a chance to do a wonderful project about our culture, our history, our people, I am eager to do it. It's important to show people who we are – we're unique, you see. It's important to restore to the black person his dignity on-screen."

beating and killing black children. But when his gardener dies in police custody, he joins the struggle against apartheid. He begins by hiring a lawyer. Euzhan wanted Marlon Brando to play the part of the lawyer. Brando, who had refused to make a movie for the previous nine years, read the script and loved it. He not only agreed to play the part, but he offered to do it for free. (Brando later accepted the union scale of $4,000 instead of his usual $1.5 million per day.)

During filming, the set was closed and the press wasn't admitted. Euzhan dealt with many other challenges. For instance, as the camera shifted between actors whose skin color varied, the image contrast on camera was too great. She solved this problem by using amber lenses to minimize skin tone differences.

With the filming of *A Dry White Season*, Euzhan became the first black female film director to make a Hollywood film. Euzhan won awards for the film from different countries, and Marlon Brando was nominated for an Academy Award for Best Supporting Actor.

After the film was released, Euzhan felt she needed a change. For a while, she had

Euzhan Palcy in Martinique with a poster for her movie *Siméon*

had enough of Hollywood, where filmmaking is a business. So she took a break in Paris because, as she put it, "in Paris, film is an art form." There, she worked on a lighter movie, *Siméon,* which collected several awards. Then she made a three-part series about the Martinique poet Aimé Césaire. And in 1994, François Mitterrand, the President of France, honored her with the Knight of the National Order of Merit for her work in film.

It wasn't long before she returned to work in Hollywood. Disney asked her to direct *Ruby Bridges,* based on the true

story, set in New Orleans, of Ruby Bridges, one of the first black children to attend a white school. Because of the story it told, Euzhan wanted to direct the film. When *Ruby Bridges* was completed, President Bill Clinton introduced the film at its debut.

Soon after, Paramount asked Euzhan to direct *The Killing Yard,* a movie for television about the Attica prison riot. Although she was interested in the

Euzhan Palcy on set

story, Euzhan was uncomfortable with the fact that it was told through the eyes of a "white man" lawyer. However, she felt the story was powerful, and ultimately she agreed. She said, "I just want human beings, without any color."

For two years, Euzhan prepared to make *The Killing Yard*. During those years she was offered two feature films that she had to turn down, but she needed that time to rework the script with the screenwriter. Euzhan, who felt there was too much dialogue, wanted to follow the saying, "show, don't tell." She worked on telling the story through visuals. For example, in the courtroom scenes, she emphasized the story of the witnesses through her film techniques, not just by the words they said. Euzhan preferred this method, which required the viewer to put together the clues of what had happened.

During prep time, Euzhan met with Alan Alda who was to play the lead. He loved the story but he had a problem with his part. He didn't want to appear as "the great white hope." As this was also a concern for Euzhan, they worked together to revise the script.

Another challenge of the script was the many courtroom scenes. Because there were so many witnesses, Euzhan was concerned that the scenes might appear monotonous. She solved the problem by working with her director of photography. They decided to move the camera around to give the shots more rhythm, they made sure that no shots were repeated, and they worked to find ways to make each shot fresh, by looking for little details.

In planning how to shoot the riot sequences, Euzhan considered using three 16-mm cameras and filming in black and white. She wanted this part to look like newsreel footage. The studio reacted strongly, however, because they didn't want that sequence in black and white. But Euzhan begged them to trust her, saying it was only a small part of the movie, and she got her way.

Euzhan Palcy on set

The riot scene required 1,200 people, gunfire, and tear gas. The problem was the budget only allowed for one hundred people. She put out the word on the radio that she was offering two free screenings of her movies. At the same time, she was working with black organizations, and when people asked what they could do to help, she told them that she needed extras, but that she didn't have a big budget. People came, and the studio provided costumes, food, and made donations to the organizations.

Euzhan believes that rehearsal time is very important, partly because many actors are vulnerable and need time to get to know and trust each other. Ultimately, there needs to be respect among all those on set – from actors to crew. Euzhan made the storyboards and then went over every shot with the crew and cast, so that they would know what every camera was doing.

Sometimes members of the cast asked specific questions about the Attica riot, and Euzhan didn't have the answers. Benita, the screenwriter, had done eight years of research, and Euzhan wanted the studio to send Benita to a rehearsal. When she found out that the studio never allowed writers on the set, she persisted, saying Benita would know the answers and that it was a matter of saving time. The studio gave in.

When filming began, Euzhan realized that the expression of such raw emotion during the shoot was taking a toll on the actors. So she asked the crew to clap every time an emotional scene was finished. The first time this happened, the actors were moved to tears.

When the shooting of the riot scene began, a spirit of cooperation developed on set. The extras worked well with the volunteers. And whenever Euzhan needed to do another take, she took time to explain why. Even though she had only twenty-three days to shoot the whole film, she knew it was worthwhile to spend extra time with the cast, and she picked the right moments to do so. The riot scene was shot in three days, after weeks of preparation.

The Killing Yard was screened at the Toronto International Film Festival to great acclaim. Euzhan continued to work on new film projects, including *The Third Lady*, an action comedy, and *Midnight's Last Ride*, a dramatic comedy starring Ellen Burstyn and Sam Shepard.

As a black filmmaker and a woman, Euzhan believes it's easier today to find work in television and in the independent world of filmmaking. However, she likes to collaborate with film studios in ways that challenge racist assumptions and stereotypes. She says, "They go like robots: straight by the book. Someone of color needs to be in the room to say, "'What about a black actor here? Some color here?' Sometimes they just never thought about it. They need to be reprogrammed. So I'm working with them. Maybe we'll each learn another way to go."

Euzhan sums up her work by saying, "I believe strongly that filmmakers have a responsibility. We can change the world. We can show people a situation – shed light on it without preaching."

MIRA NAIR

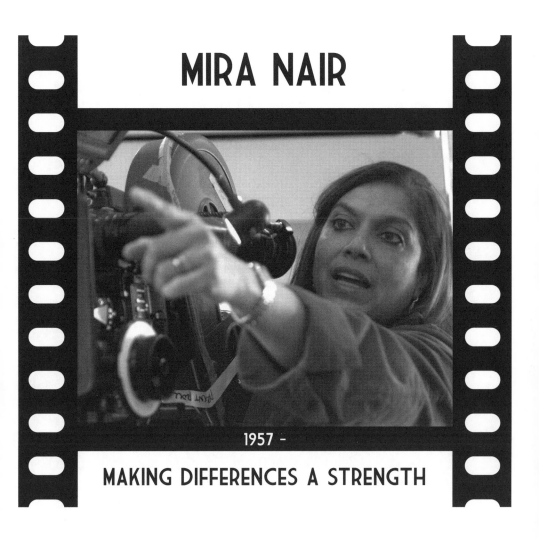

1957 –

MAKING DIFFERENCES A STRENGTH

When Mira Nair was offered the chance to direct the fifth Harry Potter film, she turned it down, even though she felt that it was a great honor. "I could think of numerous other directors who could do the job," she said. Mira needs to be "totally obsessed" with the story in order to make a film. She feels she's better suited to directing human emotion than special effects.

Born in 1957 in Bhubaneswar, India, Mira saw many Indian films as a child, since that was what most theaters offered. The only Hollywood film she saw was *Dr. Zhivago*.

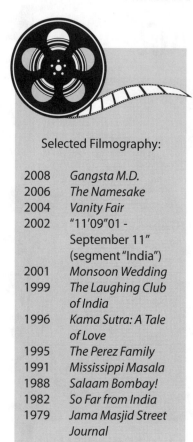

Selected Filmography:

2008	*Gangsta M.D.*
2006	*The Namesake*
2004	*Vanity Fair*
2002	*"11'09"01 - September 11"* (segment "India")
2001	*Monsoon Wedding*
1999	*The Laughing Club of India*
1996	*Kama Sutra: A Tale of Love*
1995	*The Perez Family*
1991	*Mississippi Masala*
1988	*Salaam Bombay!*
1982	*So Far from India*
1979	*Jama Masjid Street Journal*

Although Mira loved going to see films, where she felt totally immersed in other people's lives, she had no thoughts of becoming a filmmaker herself. She studied sociology at Delhi University and became involved with street theater, but she had the feeling that she was still searching for what to do with her life.

She found her calling after moving to the United States to study theater at Harvard University. She felt that the theater program was too traditional for her, so she switched her studies to documentary filmmaking. There were three students from India in her undergraduate year, and one of them, Sooni Taraporevala, later became Mira's collaborator.

On a visit back to India, Mira picked up a camera and walked through the streets of Delhi, filming. The footage records everyone's reaction to this woman who could speak their language, but had a camera in front of her face instead of a veil. She was someone "who was from there and yet not from there," she says. Back at school, her friends talked her into adding narration to her film, *Jama Masjid Street Journal*, but she later regretted it. Her first lesson in filmmaking, she says, was to hold fast to her own idea of the film, no matter how much she wanted to please those around her. She promised herself that from then on she'd follow her instincts.

After graduating, Mira moved to New York. By day she worked as a waitress and by night she edited medical films and wrote proposals for movies she wanted to make. She was interested in the lives of ordinary people, and wanted to capture their lives visually. She decided she needed to stand out, not blend in. "I made my difference my strength," she said. "You know: 'I am an Indian woman who has access to worlds that you will never have access to.'" She was given grant money to make a documentary about an Indian newspaper seller in the New York subway who visits his pregnant wife in India. Called *So Far From India*, the film won awards, and Mira began work on her next project.

Over the next five years, she made two more documentaries, but began to feel that documentaries no longer offered the challenge she was seeking. "It's as boring as sin sometimes!" she said. "You know, for four days you're not getting anything, then suddenly, it comes. You get something and it's an epiphany! But I was getting tired of waiting for things to happen and wanted to *make* them happen." Mira wanted to choose what happened to the character, the light, the mood, even the actor's clothing. She also felt that feature films had more power to change the world than documentaries, partly because of the greater number of people who watch features.

Mira decided she had to make a feature film. Even though she had no script, she contacted Sooni and some other colleagues and asked them to meet her in Bombay. On an earlier trip, an idea had come to her when her taxi was stopped at a light. She had noticed a boy who had no legs. She gave him some money and he "pirouetted flamboyantly around on the skateboard and clasped his hands above his head as if he were accepting the applause of multitudes." The image had stuck with her and now she was back to make a film about people on the fringe, especially people who had gone through a difficult experience and had found a way to develop such flamboyance and humor.

Mira and her friends put the word out on the streets of

Bombay that they were looking for kids to do some acting. Any kids who were interested in participating could audition, and those selected would take part in a workshop and the film.

On the first day, 130 children showed up. Mira chose twenty-four of them to take the workshop. The crew hung out and played cards with the street kids to get to know them and earn their trust. They were training the kids for the movie, but they also wanted to give them a feeling of self-worth. Mira made sure that the kids were paid enough to get along from day to day, but she put most of their salaries in trust until they turned twenty-one.

For a couple of months, the kids danced, did mime, sang and played theater games. They were told that the training would be like a job: they had to be there six days a week, from nine in the morning to six in the evening, and any latecomers would be fined. The kids took the workshop very seriously. Some had to come on foot from long distances, often in the heavy rains. Not one of them had a watch – and not one of them was ever late. They loved learning so much that they asked if they could come on Sundays too. Mira and Sooni went away and wrote a script about an eleven-year-old boy who is forced onto the streets after being abandoned by his parents.

Since the children couldn't read, Mira and the crew had to read out their lines. The kids improvised scenes in the workshops, often improving the dialogue, and then acted them out on video to see themselves on film. Every evening after working with the kids, Mira wondered how she was going to find funding for the film. Investors kept changing their minds. "Everybody who gives you money wants some sort of pound of flesh," Mira commented.

Salaam Bombay! was Mira's first feature, and she felt an "exquisite terror" as she had to organize one hundred crew members each morning, work in 120 degree heat, and be ready to change plans in an instant. Since they were on such a low budget, they shot on the streets, not in the studio like most Indian movie makers. Certain scenes

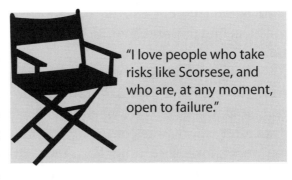

"I love people who take risks like Scorsese, and who are, at any moment, open to failure."

were supposed to be filmed in the rain, and if the rain didn't come, they had to pay for a rain machine. Every exterior scene had crowds of up to 5,000 people watching from behind the ropes. They filmed on fifty-two locations in fifty-two days. Mira said, "When you are beginning, you are just mad! I was just thinking about whether I could make it to the next day. It was that kind of feeling. Not a fear or dread, but just how to carry on." There were no rules. Even though there were sometimes eighteen different setups a day, Mira had to remain flexible to what the actor needed or the situation demanded.

Flexibility was certainly what Mira required when it came to filming the climax of the film at the Ganpati Festival, which takes place in Bombay once a year. On the day of the festival, the crew stationed themselves with cameras at several locations in the crowd, as well as on top of a crane. Soon the street was crowded with masses of people, but when they saw the camera on the crane, they felt it was an insult to the gods. They threw their flip-flops at the camera and then switched to heaving rocks. The director of photography, Sandi Sissel, had already had experience with riots when she filmed in Lebanon during a conflict. "Believe me, this was real," she said. The camera was worth more than a million dollars, and the crew realized they had no choice but to stop filming. Now Mira had to come up with a new ending for the film. For a while, she couldn't decide what it would be. In the end, she focused on a quiet moment that showed how the eleven-year-old had changed, and how life can be good and bad at the same time.

Mira was invited to screen *Salaam Bombay!* at the prestigious Cannes International Film Festival. Filming was complete, but she was still editing. Time was tight. Only two days after editing was complete, *Salaam Bombay!* was rushed to Cannes for a screening. Mira recalls the moment when the lights came up after the film was over. "The people were just sobbing and crying and laughing. And the people just stood up and clapped for, I think, ten minutes. I was in tears. I was completely paralyzed. There was so much emotion in the audience. And it was truly the first audience of the film. Nobody else had seen it before. That was terrifying."

Salaam Bombay! won the 1988 Caméra d'Or Prize for the best first film, and was voted the most popular entry at the festival. Later it was nominated for an Academy Award, and Roger Ebert named it one of the year's ten best films.

In spite of her film's success, Mira almost went broke. She couldn't find a distributor in India because there were no famous stars in the film, and she hadn't shot it in a studio. "They thought I was crazy because I had shot out on the streets. But the streets of Indian cities are wonderful locations! They're wild and crazy and unpredictable." Finally Mira found a distributor, and the film played for twenty-seven weeks in Bombay, a rare, long run for India.

Salaam Bombay! changed lives. Mira used a percentage of the film's profits to establish the Salaam Baalak Trust, a non-profit organization to provide support for street and working children in India. It was a way to better the world through art. But Mira's life was changed as well.

She began receiving film scripts from all over the world about children, India, and women. But she didn't want to make "heat and dust" films about India, she said, because she felt they showed an unreal version of India. Instead, Mira wanted to bring the cultures of the East to the West. With the idea of showing characters who – beyond traditions – are the same under their skin, Mira paired with Sooni to write *Mississippi Masala*. The story originated when Mira researched a group of people from India who were forced to leave their homes in Uganda in 1972. Many settled in faraway Mississippi, but they longed for Africa, which for them was home. At the same time, many African-Americans living in the South felt Africa was their home, though most had never been there.

When Mira searched for funding, everyone told her that interracial love stories didn't make money. "I got so used to rejection of this kind that I felt I must be doing something right." When she was raising money, potential backers asked if she could add at least one white main character. "I assured them," she says with a giggle, "that all the waiters would be white." Over time Mira was able to raise enough funds.

Denzel Washington, who starred in *Mississippi Masala*, gave Sooni and Mira helpful feedback. He recognized that they knew about the lives of people in the Indian community of Mississippi, but he felt they needed to add more details about the black community. Mira knew he was right and followed his suggestions.

Not only was Mira unfamiliar with the culture of African-Americans, she was unfamiliar with Africa. She made a trip to Uganda to do research, not knowing that it would become her home. She fell in love with the country and with her consultant, Professor Mahmood Mamdani. Mira married Mahmood while shooting in Uganda, and Kampala became her permanent home, although she lived in New York for part of the year.

Released in 1991, *Mississippi Masala* received a standing ovation at the Sundance Film Festival. It was a commercial success, and it also launched Denzel Washington's career.

After the birth of her son, Zohran, the following year, Mira did some work for television and then directed *The Perez Family*, which didn't do well at the box office.

At the same time, Mira had been developing *Kama Sutra: A Tale of Love.* She knew that a film about love and sex would be difficult to shoot in India, where even underwear was banned from being advertised on billboards. To get around the problem, she renamed the film "Tara and Maya" for the time during filming. Shooting was difficult. Days were hot and nights were cold. One actor got heat stroke. Some scenes involved actors and eighty elephants. In the heat of the moment, Mira resolved to make it simpler next time, although simplicity has never been a priority for her. Naveen Andrews (who plays Sayid on the television series *Lost*) was the lead. The film broke box-office earnings in Japan and the Far East.

Naveen Andrews also played the lead in Mira's next film, *My Own Country,* about an Indian doctor treating AIDS in rural Tennessee. Mira returned to the documentary form when she made *The Laughing Club of India.* Sitting in a traffic jam, back in India, she had noticed a banner for World Laughter Day. The result was a short film about a physician who started a laughing club, which invites everyone (at no cost) to laugh as a form of meditation, an antidote to our fast-paced lives.

Meanwhile, Mira's own life was very fast-paced. She was teaching at Columbia University, and during a lecture she challenged herself and her students to film in a different way. A group of Danish filmmakers, Dogme 95, had been filming with hand-held cameras, without adding any additional props,

"My job is to provoke you into something, into re-examining something, or looking at something differently."

dubbed music, or special lighting. It was a more pure way of filming, with an emphasis on story and performance rather than on big production values. Mira decided to make a film in the same natural way, using minimal funds and resources.

It was a tall order, but she was used to working quickly and on a low budget. She wanted to prove to herself that she could do it. Filming for *Monsoon Wedding* began in the heat of Delhi. In thirty days they had filmed the whole story using a handheld camera to show the pulsing of Indian life.

But when Mira returned to the U.S. to edit the film, she found that 300 minutes of film had been damaged by a New York airport X-ray machine. Almost five full days of shooting had been destroyed, including the climactic scene of a poolside party. Mira thought of calling everyone back for a re-shoot, but the cast and crew were already busy on new projects of their own. *Monsoon Wedding* looked doomed. Mira took another look at the damaged film and detected a blue glow in some of the shots. It might be possible to use some of the footage. Then she found out that they would receive insurance to cover the cost of another shoot, back in India. Three months later she managed to restage four scenes, as well as film the monsoon rains that had begun.

Monsoon Wedding became one of the highest-grossing foreign films in history. At the Venice Film Festival, Mira was the first woman in its history to win the Golden Lion Award.

The film screened at the Toronto International Film Festival only a few hours before the tragic events of 9/11. Mira's thought when she learned of the horrible event was that she just wanted to be in her New York apartment with her husband and son close by. She was so affected by 9/11 that she joined ten other directors to make a film in which each director's segment was exactly 11 minutes, nine seconds, and one extra frame in length. The result was a video titled "11'09"01," released in 2002.

Mira Nair directs her actors on set in *The Namesake*.

In the meantime, Mira directed *Hysterical Blindness* for HBO, staring Uma Thurman (who received a Golden Globe for her performance), and she produced a documentary in India. Part of the reason Mira can work so quickly is that she tries to work with the same crew each time. Everyone gets used to working as a team and has a chance to develop his or her own skills.

Mira herself is always looking for ways to develop and grow in the art of filmmaking. She couldn't have found a better challenge than adapting a 900-page book for the screen. In 2004, she began work on *Vanity Fair,* based on the 19th-century novel by William Makepeace Thackeray. For almost a year, Mira collaborated with the screenwriters, e-mailing back and forth until the script was ready.

Before Mira was ready to start filming, one of the stars, Reese Witherspoon, became pregnant. They needed to move the schedule forward. Mira wanted to film in England, but the budget wouldn't allow it. Then Reese donated part of her salary, and filming began on location in England.

England was a new location for Mira, and the story might seem as different from *Salaam Bombay!* as the earth is from the moon. Reese plays a character who is an outsider in society, a woman of low birth who wants to climb the heights of society in the mid-1800s. "She was somebody who didn't care for the cards that society had dealt her and she made her own deck," Mira said. *Vanity Fair* was released to mixed critical reviews. Some critics weren't satisfied with the adaptation of Thackeray's novel.

Despite the criticism, Mira went on to make another adaptation. On a long flight to India, she had read *The Namesake,* by Jhumpa Lahiri. The plot involves a couple who move from India to New York City, where their American-born son, Gogol, refuses to acknowledge his heritage or traditions. At a crucial moment, he brings his traditions back into his life. Mira's old friend Sooni adapted the novel into a screenplay, which was shot on location in India and in New York. Released in 2007, *The Namesake* struck a chord with viewers and reviewers alike.

Mira continues to bring very human stories to the screen. Her short film *Migration* was screened at the 2007 Toronto International Film Festival to raise awareness about AIDS in India, and she is currently working on *Gangsta M.D.*, starring Chris Tucker, and *Shantaram,* with Johnny Depp.

For Mira, filmmaking is not just about making movies. One of her aims is to show women on screen as they are in real life – multi-dimensional. "There is so much still for us to say," Mira comments. "Women have not yet been given the time of day in terms of film." She believes that her work should include giving back to the community. After living in Uganda for eleven years, Mira recognized that many African filmmakers were unable to make movies. She started up an annual film workshop, Maisha, for aspiring East African and South Asian filmmakers. They study screenwriting, directing, cinematography, editing, and sound mixing to tell their stories – and they produce them locally. Spike Lee and Sophia Coppola are on the advisory committee.

When asked to advise young filmmakers, Mira says, "A director should be a person who eats up the world." By this she means traveling, writing, and reading, but it also means being a sponge – watching and absorbing everything. Mira believes that everyone's particular traits and abilities are their strengths. "Don't smooth the rough edges of your own personality or interests. Develop them," she says.

PATRICIA ROZEMA

1958 –

TELLING TRUTH THROUGH FICTION

You would think that anyone who turned out to be a film-maker would have been steeped in movies since childhood. But until she was sixteen, Patricia Rozema had seen only one movie: *Snow White*. Patricia grew up in a Calvinist family. Her parents had left Holland after World War II, and settled in Canada where Patricia was born, in Kingston, Ontario, in 1958. They took their daughter to chapel every day, and although they were more open-minded than some Calvinists, Patricia's parents shielded her from the influences of television and movies.

Selected Filmography:

2008	*Grey Gardens*
2000	*Happy Days*
1999	*Mansfield Park*
1997	"Six Gestures" from series *Yo-Yo Ma, Inspired by Bach*
1995	*When Night Is Falling*
1990	*White Room*
1987	*I've Heard the Mermaids Singing*
1985	"Passion: A Letter in 16mm"

Patricia was a storyteller almost from the time she could talk. And apparently people liked to listen to her. She acted in school plays in grade one; in grade two, when her teacher had to step out of the room, she asked Patricia to tell the class a story while she was gone.

When she was sixteen, Patricia went on a date with a "Canadian" boy – which meant he was someone outside the church. That's when she saw her second movie. Her friend took her to see *The Exorcist*. She had nightmares for weeks, but she started to see her life and the church differently. She began to rebel against those who came between her and what she wanted to do.

Patricia went to Calvin College in Michigan and graduated with a degree in philosophy and English, and a minor in journalism. Then she started to think about how she could "make a living telling stories." After working as an intern in television, she applied for a job at the Canadian Broadcasting Corporation (CBC). When she didn't hear back from the CBC, she kept calling until they finally gave her an interview. "I have no shame if I want something," she says.

Patricia did land a job with *The Journal*, a CBC television news program, but she found the work frustrating and soon realized that journalism wasn't for her. News stories deal with facts, but the storyteller in Patricia longed to transform the facts into stories. She wanted to let the audience "walk a few steps in someone else's shoes." She felt that by directing films, she could slip inside the soul of each character in a way that only fiction can do. "In fact," she says, "by telling fiction, you can tell more of the truth."

It wasn't long before she lost her job, when the CBC had to make cut-backs and lay off staff. This was a shock for her, but it also gave new direction to her life. She felt she had nothing to lose, and she began to freelance as an assistant director on several projects. She took filmmaking courses, wrote film scripts, and began to send her scripts to producers.

In 1985, Patricia received a grant to make her short film *Passion: A Letter in 16mm* – the film was like a love letter spoken to the camera. Because she was taking a five-week course in film production, she had access to the equipment required to make the film. While she was in the editing room for the first time, constructing a story with images, she suddenly thought, "Yes, I'm home." Her film was released in 1985 and won a prize at the Chicago International Film Festival.

Patricia continued working as an assistant director, including on David Cronenberg's film *The Fly*. At the same time, she began writing a script for a feature film. The experience of making her short film had taught her that a film script needs to have fewer words and more visuals.

Patricia began to raise funds for her feature film *I've Heard the Mermaids Singing*. Even though *Passion: A Letter in 16mm* had been successful (which definitely helped in fundraising), Patricia acknowledged that she and her co-producer, Alex

"I really do believe we come to films for the same reason we go to religion: We want stories that tell us there is order. Although there's conflict, we come out okay in the end. That's really what we want, again and again, on a sophisticated or a simple level."

Raffé, just didn't know how to go about raising private funding. She said, "You can't imagine how ignorant we were."

But in the end they succeeded, and filming began. *I've Heard the Mermaids Singing* is a comedy about Polly, a disorganized, shy woman who discovers art fraud at the gallery where she works. Throughout the film, Polly keeps a video diary of things that happen to her. Polly, played by Sheila McCarthy, transforms herself from a bumbling, awkward, young woman into an accomplished artist. Once she is no longer an outsider, she feels that she's participating in life. She stops judging herself and begins to trust her own visions and perceptions. The movie ends, as it began, with Polly speaking to her video camera. Patricia said that filming is "not about angles or dollies, but emotions – and characters like Polly."

Patricia had taken a rough script and turned it into a film in eighteen months – on a ridiculously small budget of $350,000. But amazingly, when *I've Heard the Mermaids Singing* was finished, she was invited to screen the film at the famous Cannes International Film Festival. Patricia worried that people might walk out. But in fact, when the film ended, the audience rose and gave her a rare ten-minute standing ovation, complete with hoots and hollers. That year (1987), Patricia received the festival's New Director Award. She was only twenty-nine years old, and this was a life-changing moment for her.

After the award ceremony Patricia had dinner with members of the press. She decided to ask one of them to tell her what he thought were the film's weaknesses. But after listening to his list of the movie's shortcomings, she went into the bathroom and cried her eyes out. One thing was certain: She would have to get used to critics if she wanted to make films. Her goal was to tell a story honestly, and to make films that touch people, but trying to satisfy the critics would be futile. She would need to find ways to protect herself. At Cannes she began to understand one of the reasons sunglasses are associated with stardom – they protect actors from making eye contact with others.

Patricia's next challenge was to find a distributor for her film. Harvey Weinstein, who had had formed Miramax, was so interested in *I've Heard the Mermaids Singing* that he kept sending Patricia and Alex bottles of champagne. Then one day he made them an offer – and he told them they must make a decision before they left the room. They were new at the game and had never faced this situation before – Patricia and Alex figured this must be the way a deal is done. They accepted Weinstein's offer and sold him the rights to *Mermaids* for $500,000. The film went on to gross more than $6 million!

Patricia could now write on her passport that her profession was filmmaker. And because of her success at Cannes it was easier to raise money for her next film. However, she soon discovered that it was harder to make a second film that could equal the impact of her first. Even though she wanted to stretch herself as a filmmaker, the thought of trying something very different was a bit frightening. It was hard for her to find a balance. Her next film, *White Room,* was released in 1990 and was praised as a gothic fairy tale. It won some awards, but it didn't do well. Patricia went from the top of the heap to the bottom in just three years. This was a tough lesson, and she lost her confidence.

Within a year, however, Patricia joined Canada's top filmmakers to make short films in celebration of Montreal's 350th anniversary. She directed *Desperanto (Let Sleeping Girls Lie)*, a playful short about a meek teacher, starring Sheila McCarthy, who longs to find romance during a visit to mysterious Montreal. On her last night in Montreal, she goes to a party where everyone except her speaks French. Misunderstandings occur: she thinks a handsome man is flirting with her, but he isn't. Then she sits on a strawberry and it stains her dress.

When she starts imagining what it would be like to be in control of the situation, English subtitles suddenly appear that explain the French dialogue. The character steps out of the film frame to read the subtitles. She drops one word in her blouse and another dissolves in her wine. With this quirky film, Patricia proved her belief that although "success is forgotten, originality has children."

Patricia's confidence was bolstered when she heard the news that *I've Heard the Mermaids Singing* was voted one of the top ten most popular Canadian films. She began working on her next film, *When Night is Falling*. Completed in 1995, the film was well received, and it won the Audience Award at the 1995 Berlin Film Festival. Over the next few years Patricia worked on different projects, and she had her first experience directing for television. She won a Primetime Emmy in 1998 for writing and directing "Six Gestures," part of the series *Yo-Yo Ma, Inspired by Bach*.

In 1999, Harvey Weinstein (from Miramax) approached Patricia with an adaptation of Jane Austen's novel *Mansfield Park*. She read the script and decided to turn it down – too boring, she felt. When Weinstein asked if she wanted to rewrite it, Patricia spent seven months writing in solitude.

Her main challenge was to figure out how to capture on film the quiet and passive character of Fanny. She began by reading Jane Austen's letters and underlining everything

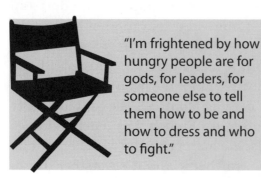

"I'm frightened by how hungry people are for gods, for leaders, for someone else to tell them how to be and how to dress and who to fight."

that "felt fabulous" to her. She decided to add two layers to the story. One layer portrayed Fanny as a writer – and in the film, Fanny reads letters and stories that were actually written by Jane Austen. The second gave Fanny's character more depth and playfulness, by having Fanny read Austen's words directly to the camera.

For Patricia, fiction allows for "the creation of all possible worlds," and reading fiction helps her write film adaptations. When writing, Patricia tries to maintain the tone of the story, so it sounds like it's being made up in the moment. One example occurs in *Mansfield Park,* when Fanny tries to explain to Sir Thomas why she refuses to marry Henry. Fanny says, "He is not without charm, but like many charming people he conceals an almost absolute dependence on the appreciation of others." This line sounds like Jane Austen, but it was actually written by Patricia.

Patricia submitted the script to Miramax and it was accepted right away. With Lesley Barber, her partner, and Jacoba, her daughter, Patricia moved to England for filming.

She was the first woman to direct a Jane Austen movie,

Patricia Rozema with Harold Pinter on set in *Mansfield Park*

Patricia directs her actors on set.

and was given an unusually high budget (for a film of this kind) of $16 million to work with. Patricia said that directing such a huge project was "like driving an ocean liner, no quick turns . . . a sense of stability." Patricia filmed many of the shots close in because she wanted to show the humanity of the characters; that style of filming also made the film a more modern interpretation. Many critics called *Mansfield Park* one of the best film adaptations of a Jane Austen novel.

On set, Patricia's style was to ask questions whenever she didn't know something. She felt it was more embarrassing to pretend to know something, and then get it wrong, than to ask for help. However, she also never doubts that she has what it takes to do the job well.

Patricia had an unexpected hurdle to negotiate when she finished filming *Mansfield Park*. She was asked to cut a scene of Fanny looking at sketches of slaves being tortured. If she didn't, she would lose the PG-13 rating in the U.S. But it was an important scene for Patricia, and she refused to budge. In the end, she made a deal that if she cut a shot of nudity, she could keep the rest of the scene. As a result, U.S. audiences see the cut version; most other countries show the movie in its complete form.

Patricia obviously thrives on variety. During the next few years she directed a number of film shorts, such as *Happy Days*, based on a Samuel Beckett play in which a woman is buried up to her neck in dirt. The film was included in *Beckett on Film: 19 Films x 19 Directors*. She directed an HBO series *Tell Me You Love Me*, which many critics say pushes the boundaries of television. She has also worked on a musical, and a feature film, *Grey Gardens*, starring Drew Barrymore and Jessica Lange.

Patricia encourages women to write stories and to direct. Although writing doesn't have the glamour, and is not as well rewarded, she believes it is more creative and often has the real power. She advises filmmakers to make a film with personality with a kernel of an idea and then fighting to keep that spark in the film. However, she warns that there are many bitter people working in the field. "You must do everything you can to avoid bitterness because with bitterness you're dead – everything's dead." Patricia believes that the only way to make unusual films is to stay open emotionally and to separate the film industry from the act of filmmaking.

Patricia thinks that filmmakers are much more affected by their education and background than by whether they are male or female. Even when she worked on sets where there were mostly men, she didn't have trouble as a woman. However, she says, "I believe that women have been held back unnaturally and unjustly. It's tragic what the world has lost."

Inspiration for making films can come from many places, but for Patricia it comes from writers she respects, and from music, which she listens to for the tone. She believes that a film director is in charge of the tone of a film and "music conveys that more effectively than anything."

Patricia says that being a director is physically demanding, but if a filmmaker has only this one "little god-given moment – Zeus-given moment – to create something magical" it's very important to do only the projects that give you energy, and to do stories that come from a special place. "You close your eyes and think of a movie and make it." And then when a film is done, Patricia says, "there's a very distinct rush I feel when I see the pictures move before my eyes the way they did behind my eyelids."

GLOSSARY

arc: a character arc shows how a character changes throughout the story

director: the one who runs the set – composes the shots, creates the movements, uses sound and music, paces scenes and tells the story visually

director of photography: helps the director plan the shots and set-ups, responsible for lighting each shot, responsible for the look of the film, decides on lenses and camera settings

docu-drama: documentaries with scenes of what it might have been like if it had been filmed, made with a script and actors

documentary: a film of fact, or non-fiction, not using actors but the people involved in the event

editor: a person who cuts and connects shots to form a sequence of events

filmmaker: someone who makes films for the cinema or television

genre: a category of film or writing

handheld camera: camera that's compact enough to be held in the hand – the film is usually shakier than that produced by a feature film camera

producer: the boss of the film – usually the one who finds the funds to make the film, often brings the participants of the film together, including the writer, director and cast

protagonist: the main character in a drama

scenario: name for screenplay in early days of filming

shot list: how the scene would be shot, including the angle, the content in the frame, and whether it's a close-up, medium or long shot

16 mm camera: more portable and less expensive than 35-mm cameras, it is was used in news reporting and for shooting outside organized production sets

storyboard: drawings used as visual aids, usually prepared by the director with help from the art director – some directors do one for every scene and every shot – important for complicated action scenes

treatment: a short description of a screenplay

two-reeler: two reels of film from the silent era, each about 12 to 16 minutes long

SOURCES
AND RESOURCES

NELL SHIPMAN

Acker, Ally. *Reel Women: Pioneers of the Cinema, 1896 to the Present.*
New York: Continuum International Publishing Group, 1991

Armatage, Kay. *The Girl from God's Country: Nell Shipman and the Silent
Cinema.* Toronto: University of Toronto Press, 2003

Lucas, Ralph. "Biography of Nell Shipman." 2002 www.northernstars.
ca/actorsstu/shipman.html

Shipman, Nell. *The Silent Screen and My Talking Heart: An Autobiography.*
3rd ed. Boise, Idaho: Boise State University Press, 2001

Boise State University, Idaho, www.boisestate.edu/hemingway/ifc/nell.
html

University of Toronto, www.utoronto.ca/shipman

Quotes from *The Silent Screen and My Talking Heart: An Autobiography,*
Nell Shipman, 2001, reprinted by permission of the publisher, Boise
State University Press

IDA LUPINO

Acker, Ally. *Reel Women: Pioneers of the Cinema, 1896 to the Present.*
New York: Continuum International Publishing Group, 1991

Donati, William. *Ida Lupino: A Biography.* Lexington: The University
Press of Kentucky, 1996

Quart, Barbara Koenig. *Women Directors: The Emergence of a New Cinema.* New York: Praeger, 1988

Quotes reprinted by permission of the publishers: *Reel Women: Pioneers of the Cinema, 1896 to the Present.* Acker, Ally, 1991, Continuum International Publishing Group; TV Guide, October 8, 1966; and *Ida Lupino: A Biography,* Donati, William, The University Press of Kentucky

MARGARETHE VON TROTTA

Acker, Ally. *Reel Women: Pioneers of the Cinema, 1896 to the Present.* New York: Continuum International Publishing Group, 1991

Kaplan, E. Ann. *Women & Film: Both Sides of the Camera.* New York: Methuen, 1993

Quart, Barbara Koenig. *Women Directors: The Emergence of a New Cinema.* New York: Praeger, 1988

Stone, Judy. *Eye on the World: Conversations with International Filmmakers.* Los Angeles CA: Silman-James Press, 1997

Quotes reprinted by permission of the publishers: *Reel Women: Pioneers of the Cinema, 1896 to the Present.* Acker, Ally, 1991, Continuum International Publishing Group

ANNE WHEELER

Beard, William and White, Jerry. *North of Everything English-Canadian Cinema Since 1980.* Edmonton: University of Alberta Press, 2002

Cole, Janis and Holly Dale. *Calling the Shots: Profiles of Women Filmmakers.* Kingston, Ontario: Quarry Press,1993

Melnyk, George. *One Hundred Years of Canadian Cinema.* Toronto: University of Toronto Press, 2004

Monk, Katherine. *Weird Sex & Snowshoes: And other Canadian Film Phenomena.* Vancouver: Raincoast Books, 2001

www.northernstars.ca/directorsmz/wheeler.html

RESOURCES

Anne Wheeler's website www.annewheeler.com

Some quotes from Suzanne Simoni interview with Anne Wheeler, December 2006

MARTHA COOLIDGE
Acker, Ally. *Reel Women: Pioneers of the Cinema, 1896 to the Present.* New York: Continuum International Publishing Group, 1991

Beard, William and White, Jerry. *North of Everything English-Canadian Cinema Since 1980.* Edmonton: University of Alberta Press, 2002

Cole, Janis and Holly Dale. *Calling the Shots: Profiles of Women Filmmakers.* Kingston, Ontario: Quarry Press, 1993

Martha Coolidge, Director
http://www.pbs.org/wgbh/masterpiece/americancollection/ponder/coolidge.html

Quart, Barbara Koenig. *Women Directors: The Emergence of a New Cinema.* New York: Praeger, 1988

Tribute.ca Director Bio http://www.tribute.ca/bio.asp?id=11842

Martha Coolidge's Website www.marthacoolidge.com

Quotes reprinted by permission of the publishers: *Reel Women: Pioneers of the Cinema, 1896 to the Present.* Acker, Ally, 1991, Continuum International Publishing Group; *Calling the Shots: Profiles of Women Filmmakers.* Cole, Janis and Holly Dale, 1993, Quarry Press

SALLY POTTER
Boorman, John, Luddy, Tom, Thomson, David, and Donahue, Walter (Ed.). *Projections 4: Film-makers on Film-making.* London, U.K.: Faber and Faber, 1995

Donahue, Walter, the film's story editor. "Immortal Longing." *Sight and Sound*, March 1993

MacDonald, Scott. *A Critical Cinema 3: Interviews with Independent*

Filmmakers. University of California Press: Berkeley and L.A., 1998

Potter, Sally. "Notes on the Adaptation of the Book *Orlando"* www.uah.edu/woolf/Orlando_Potter.htm

Potter, Sally. *Yes: Screenplay and Notes.* N.Y.: Newmarket Press, 2005

Stone, Judy. *Eye on the World: Conversations with International Filmmakers.* Los Angeles C.A.: Silman-James Press, 1997

Sally Potter's Website www.sallypotter.net

Quotes reprinted by permission of the publishers: "Immortal Longing." Walter Donahue, *Sight and Sound*, March 1993

DEEPA MEHTA
Cole, Janis and Holly Dale. *Calling the Shots: Profiles of Women Filmmakers.* Kingston, Ontario: Quarry Press, 1993

Levitin, Jacqueline. "Deepa Mehta as a Transnational Filmmaker, or You Can't Go Home Again." In *North of Everything: English-Canadian Cinema since 1980.* Edited by William Beard and Jerry White. Edmonton: University of Alberta Press, 2002

Banning, Kass. "Excerpts from a Master Class with Deepa Mehta." In *Women Filmmakers: Refocusing.* Edited by Jacqueline Levitin, Judith Plessis, and Valerie Raoul. Vancouver: UBC Press, 2002

Monk, Katherine. *Weird Sex & Snowshoes: And other Canadian Film Phenomena.* Vancouver: Raincoast Books, 2001

The Hollywood.com Guide to Film Directors, Ed. Staff of Hollywood.com. N.Y.: Carroll and Graf Publishers, 2004

http://www.canadianfilmencyclopedia.ca/

Quotes reprinted by permission of the publishers: *Calling the Shots: Profiles of Women Filmmakers.* Cole, Janis and Holly Dale, 1993, Quarry Press

RESOURCES

EUZHAN PALCY

Acker, Ally. *Reel Women: Pioneers of the Cinema, 1896 to the Present.* New York: Continuum Internationaal Publishing Group, 1991

Cole, Janis and Holly Dale. *Calling the Shots: Profiles of Women Filmmakers.* Kingston, Ontario: Quarry Press, 1993

Foster, Gwendolyn Audrey. *Women Filmmakers of the African & Asian Diaspora: Decolonizing the Gaze, Locating Subjectivity.* Carbondale and Edwardsville: Southern Illinois University Press, 1997

Quart, Barbara Koenig. *Women Directors: The Emergence of a New Cinema.* New York: Praeger, 1988

Stone, Judy. *Eye on the World: Conversations with International Filmmakers.* Los Angeles CA: Silman-James Press, 1997

Euzhan Palcy Website http://www.euzhanpalcy.com/ephome3.html

Quotes reprinted by permission of the publishers: *Reel Women: Pioneers of the Cinema, 1896 to the Present.* Acker, Ally, 1991, Continuum International Publishing Group; *Calling the Shots: Profiles of Women Filmmakers.* Cole, Janis and Holly Dale, 1993, Quarry Press

MIRA NAIR

Cole, Janis and Holly Dale. *Calling the Shots: Profiles of Women Filmmakers.* Kingston, Ontario: Quarry Press, 1993

Muir, John Kenneth, *Mercy in her Eyes: The Films of Mira Nair.* New York: Applause Theatre & Cinema Books, 2006

Lowenstein, Stephen Ed. *My First Movie.* London: Faber and Faber, 2000

Redding, Judith M. and Brownworth, Victoria A. *Film Fatales: Independent Women Filmmakers.* Seattle: Seal Press, 1997

Stone, Judy. *Eye on the World: Conversations with International Filmmakers.* Los Angeles CA: Silman-James Press, 1997

Mira Nair's Website: http://www.mirabaifilms.com/articles.html

Quotes reprinted by permission of the publishers: *Calling the Shots: Profiles of Women Filmmakers.* Cole, Janis and Holly Dale, 1993, Quarry Press; *My First Movie.* Lowenstein, Stephen, Ed., Faber and Faber, 2000

PATRICIA ROZEMA
Acker, Ally. *Reel Women: Pioneers of the Cinema, 1896 to the Present.* New York: Continuum International Publishing Group, 1991

Beard, William and White, Jerry. *North of Everything English-Canadian Cinema Since 1980.* Edmonton: University of Alberta Press, 2002

Cole, Janis and Dale, Holly. *Calling the Shots: Profiles of Women Filmmakers.* Kingston, Ontario: Quarry Press, 1993

Lowenstein, Stephen, Ed. *My First Movie.* London: Faber and Faber, 2000

Melnyk, George. *One Hundred Years of Canadian Cinema.* Toronto: University of Toronto Press, 2004

Monk, Katherine. *Weird Sex and Snowshoes.* Vancouver: Raincoast Books, 2001

Quotes reprinted by permission of the publishers: *Reel Women: Pioneers of the Cinema, 1896 to the Present.* Acker, Ally, 1991, Continuum International Publishing Group; *My First Movie.* Lowenstein, Stephen, Ed., Faber and Faber, 2000. Additional quotes from Suzanne Simoni interview with Patricia Rozema, December 2006

PHOTO CREDITS

NELL SHIPMAN
All photos courtesy Special Collections, Boise State University, Albertsons Library (Boise, Idaho)

IDA LUPINO
Page 25: © Bettmann/Corbis
Page 20: © John Springer Collection/Corbis
Page 22: © American Memory, Moving Image Section, Motion Picture, Broadcasting and Recorded Sound Division
Page 26: © Alan Light

MARGARETHE VON TROTTA
All photos © Nils Bremer

ANNE WHEELER
All photos courtesy Anne Wheeler

MARTHA COOLIDGE
Page 51: © Marcel Hartmann/Sygma/Corbis

SALLY POTTER
All photos © Sally Potter and Adventure Pictures

DEEPA MEHTA
Page 69: © Toronto Star/Rene Johnston
Page 76: © Toronto Star/ Vince Talotta

EUZHAN PALCY
Page 79: © Euzhan Palcy
Page 85: © Giraud Phillipe/Corbis/Sygma
Page 86: © Euzhan Palcy
Page 88: © G. Zobda

MIRA NAIR
All photos courtesy Fox Searchlight Pictures

PATRICIA ROZEMA
All photos courtesy Patricia Rozema